## WHAT DO YOUR DREAMS MEAN?

Hundreds of dream subjects—and their meaning for YOU—are listed in this fascinating book. Since one third of your life is spent asleep, the events that occur in your dreams are vitally important to your present—and your future! Discover how to interpret the secret life of your dreams and get a new, valuable insight into your *real* personality.

## WAKE UP TO NEW AWARENESS OF THE "INNER YOU" WITH

## THE COMPLETE DREAM BOOK

# THE COMPLETE
# DREAM
# BOOK

### Edward Frank Allen

**WARNER BOOKS**

A Time Warner Company

Dreams do come true
and so this book is dedicated to
MISS MARGARET BYRNES
who suggested it

WARNER BOOKS EDITION

Copyright 1938, renewal © 1966 by Edward Frank Allen
All rights reserved.

This Warner Books Edition is published by arrangement with
J. B. Lippincott Company, subsidiary of Harper & Row Inc.,
East Washington Square, Philadelphia, Pennsylvania 19105

Warner Books, Inc.
1271 Avenue of the Americas
New York, N.Y. 10020

Ⓦ A Time Warner Company

Printed in the United States of America

First Printing: December, 1967

25   24   23

## CONTENTS

# INTRODUCTION

Dreaming is thinking in sleep. Perhaps it is much more than that. It may be that it is the projection of the astral body out into space beyond the stars where our vision of things past and things to come is not bound by mundane restrictions.

Sometimes we are pleased with what we see and do in dreams; at other times we are shocked, disgusted or frightened, so that we cry out in terror.

In our waking moments it is usually possible to control our thoughts, but there appears to be no method of dreaming of any certain thing at will.* In sleep the brain functions without any apparent directing force. Dreams sometimes lead into places and situations that are wholly foreign to the personality and experience of the dreamer; but all dreams must of necessity be based on knowledge, either first-hand or acquired by reading or hearsay.

Dreams may be of perfectly normal things. They may also be of highly improbable or even impossible happenings. They may reconstruct childhood days, or they may look forward to old age. Some of them are of idyllic beauty; others full of horror. They may range between love and hate, pleasure and pain, wealth and poverty, happiness and sorrow, light and darkness, heat and cold, Heaven and Hell. Dreams may be a jumble of the familiar and unfamiliar; they may be funny, sad, uncanny, religious, immoral, or just plain cockeyed.

I doubt if there is anyone who does not dream. Possibly

---

*A beautiful story in which this seems to be possible is *Peter Ibbetson*, by George DuMaurier.

idiots do not, but maybe they do. I hesitate to speak as an authority on this particular subject. There are many evidences that even dogs dream.

Aristotle, in his *History of Animals,* says: "Not only men appear to dream, but horses, oxen, sheep, goats, dogs, and all viviparous quadrupeds. Dogs show this by barking in their sleep. It is not quite clear what oviparous animals dream, but it is quite plain that they sleep. . . . Man sleeps the most of all animals. *Infants and young children do not dream at all* but dreaming begins in most at about four or five years old. There have been men and women who have never dreamt at all; sometimes such persons, when they have advanced in age, begin to dream; this has preceded a change in their body, either for death or infirmity."

On the other hand, Pliny, in his *Natural History,* has his own ideas about babies dreaming: "The infant dreams from the very first, for it will suddenly awake with every symptom of alarm, and while asleep will imitate the action of sucking."

From unremembered time people of all conditions have dreamed. There are countless references to dreams in literature, including the Bible, and in the writings of the ancient poets, historians, scientists and philosophers. Dreaming is common to all races, nationalities, times and conditions. There are dream books in English, Dutch, Arabic, French, German, Greek, Russian, Siamese, Latin, and no doubt many other languages.

Belief in the significance of dreams is nearly as old as dreams themselves. Some of the wisest and most dignified men and women have for many centuries regarded them as prophecies, portents, and omens of either good or evil, and through the ages there have been evolved from experience numerous interpretations of the dreams that human beings have.

While there is a certain amount of truth in the saying, "There is nothing new under the sun," it will have to be admitted that since Adam and Eve had their dreams in the Garden of Eden, there have been many new arrangements of things—resulting in such comparative novelties as the 'ephone, radio, phonograph, photography, airplanes, 'r cars and housekeeping trailers, streamlined trains, modern surgery, the high speed printing press, and so on through a long list.

It is easy to understand how dreams keep pace with the times, and how, with world progress, their interpretation may vary considerably. For instance, the ancient dream books did not mention motor cars. However, in one published a century or more ago, there was this entry:

"To dream of riding in a wagon without a horse portends a mystery in your life that you will be unable to solve." That sort of dream at that time would verge on the supernatural. Today it would be the most natural thing in the world to dream of riding in a wagon without a horse, and it would have no particular significance unless the automobile crashed, or unless there were some unusual feature connected with it.

Similarly, to dream of music or voices coming from an unrecognized source had an entirely different significance before the coming of the radio than it has now. This sort of dream has changed from the supernatural to the perfectly normal, and consequently it must be interpreted in an entirely different manner. Radio in a dream may be merely an adjunct, and not necessarily the dream itself. It helps to establish the kind of dream, to create the atmosphere or setting, and perhaps by the character of the program to give point to the dream.

It is quite possible that you will have one or more dreams that are not listed in this book. No book, or set of books, could cover all the subjects that might be dreamed about. Suppose you dreamed of eating *caraway seeds* and you failed to find a reference. In such a case, you might look up *eating, seeds,* and *flavor.* By interpreting each, singly and in combination, you would be likely to get the answer. If there were any outstanding conditions associated with your eating caraway seeds, such as moonlight, rain, snow, a picnic, or what not, the added interpretation of these would have a bearing on the portent.

There are likely to be two or more references for every dream. For example, if you dream of machinery, it is probable that *wheels* are an important part of the dream. Likewise, if an *automobile* figures prominently in your dream, you would also do well to look up *wheels* in

9

connection with it. If it is a large and expensive car, another reference should be *luxury*. If it is so small as to appear a child's car, *toy* might be indicated. If it is an omnibus, it might suggest *crowd*.

Naturally enough, the outstanding feature of a dream is the one with the greatest significance. There may, however, be qualifying factors in points that are incidental to it. These should be looked up and your findings carefully weighed in connection with the main theme.

There is no reason why a "bad" dream should necessarily worry the dreamer, disagreeable though it may be at the time. Some dreams of this character have excellent portents, while others, of unhappy augury, may be regarded as warnings that will help to avoid danger. Remember Henley's inspiring lines:

> "I am the master of my fate,
> I am the captain of my soul."*

*Invictus,* by William Ernest Henley.

# WHAT DO MY DREAMS MEAN

# CHAPTER I

Dreams may mean much. On the other hand, they may mean little; and they may mean nothing. There are different kinds of dreams, and there are different conditions under which they occur. It is easy to see why this is so, for under the exciting or otherwise stimulating influence of unusual events, the mind, even during waking hours, reacts in a strange manner.

For instance, a sleep induced by laughing gas, or nitrous oxide, frequently produces curious results. It has even had the effect of making the most modest and gentle young ladies burst out into tirades of profanity, which would bring the blush of shame to the cheek of a longshoreman.

Laughing gas produced the following authentic dream— interesting as an index of the way the mind works, but of no significance so far as prophecy goes. A patient in a dentist's office asked to have a tooth extracted. He was given the gas, went to sleep with the peculiar *tightening* sensation usual with this gas, and dreamed that he was in a great room. He rose to a height close to the ceiling, and began to soar around the room close to the walls. Suddenly he saw a huge hook protruding from the side wall, and he found himself going toward it. He opened his mouth to scream; the hook caught one of his teeth with an awful wrench. He felt himself falling; and he became conscious as the dentist was saying, "That was a big one!" Obviously it would be foolish to look up *dentist* and *hook* in the dream book for such a dream at this.

Other dreams which mean nothing are those resulting from over-indulgence of one kind or another—too much rich food or drink,* drugs, fatigue, or mental exhaustion. The nightmare induced by mince pie is not a valid dream, so far as prophecy is concerned, nor is any dream to be taken seriously if it occurs during the first part of the night, or while the digestive processes are still going on. There will be something about drug users' dreams later on.

Dreams that are brought to a termination by certain sounds that awaken you—such as the crying of a baby, the ringing of a doorbell, or the slamming of a door—may be simply nothing more than lightning thoughts that go through your mind, seeming to anticipate and have their climax in the sound that awakened you. Such dreams are to be regarded simply as psychological phenomena, or mechanically rather than spiritually induced dreams. They are frequently interesting, but they have no bearing on future events in your life.

Throughout the ages, doubtless since the time of Adam and Eve, there has been a sincere belief in the significance of dreams by people of every rank and station in life. It is not merely we ordinary persons who have this belief. Some of the greatest figures of all time, both men and women, have been influenced by their visions in sleep. Moreover, they have consulted others whom they considered expert in the interpretation of dreams.

Rudyard Kipling, one of the most highly regarded writers of the nineteenth and twentieth centuries, tells in his book of reminiscenses** of a dream that he had wherein he attended a ceremony in a large and ancient hall. He particularly noticed the stone flooring. When the ceremony was ended, someone in back of him put his hand on his arm and said, "I want a word with you."

---

*Pliny, in his *Natural History,* says "Dreams immediately after we have taken wine and food, or when we have just fallen asleep again after waking, have no meaning or value whatever."

**Something of Myself, by Rudyard Kipling. Doubleday, Doran Co.

He remembered the dream in detail. More than a month afterward he attended a ceremony in Westminster Abbey. He noticed the stone flooring, and he recognized it as that which he had seen in his dream.

And after the ceremony was over, *a man came up to him, put his hand on his arm, and said, "I want a word with you, please."*

Abraham Lincoln, revered for his wisdom and loved for his humanity, believed firmly in the significance of dreams. Shortly before his death, he told his wife and a group of friends a dream that was a premonition of tragedy. The President, it seems, was walking from room to room in the White House. He saw no one, but everywhere he heard sobbing. Finally he arrived at the east room where there was a catafalque on which there was a corpse. It was guarded by soldiers, behind whom was a crowd of weeping people.

"Who is dead in the White House?" he asked one of the guards.

"The President," came the answer; "he was assassinated." With this reply there was an outburst of grief from the crowd of people, and Mr. Lincoln awoke.

*A few days later, John Wilkes Booth fired the shot that plunged a nation into mourning.*

Lincoln had other dreams. Only a few hours before he went to Ford's Theatre, Washington, at which he was assassinated on April 4, 1865, he held his last cabinet meeting, and on this occasion he described a dream he had had the preceding night. General Ulysses S. Grant had been invited to attend the meeting, and was present. He had just arrived from Appomattox, where General Robert E. Lee had surrendered the Confederate Army on April 9, but he was worried about General Sherman, who was facing General Joseph E. Johnston's army near Goldsboro, N.C.

So Grant asked President Lincoln for news of Sherman. The President replied that a dream he had had made him believe that all was well. In the diary of Gideon Welles, Secretary of the Navy under Lincoln, the President's story of the dream was described as follows:

"The President remarked that *news would come soon and come favorably,* he had no doubt, for he had last night his usual dream, which had preceded nearly every great event of the war. We inquired the particulars of this remarkable dream. He said it was in my element—it related to the water; that he seemed to be in a singular and indescribable vessel, but always the same, and that he was moving with great rapidity toward a dark and indefinite shore; that he had had this same singular dream preceding the firing on Sumter, and battles of Bull Run, Antietam, Gettysburg, Stone River, Vicksburg, Wilmington, etc.

"General Grant remarked with some emphasis and asperity that Stone River was no victory—that a few such victories would have ruined the country and that he knew of no important results from it.

"The President said that perhaps he should not altogether agree with him, but whatever might be the facts, his singular dream preceded that fight. Victory did not always follow his dream, but the event and results were important.

"He had no doubt that a battle had taken place or was about to be fought, 'and Johnston will be beaten; for I had this strange dream again last night. It must relate to Sherman; my thoughts are in that direction, and I know of no other very important event which is likely just now to occur.'"

*A few days later General Johnston surrendered his army to General Sherman.*

\* \* \*

Dreams have influenced the world. Many of them—sent, it may be, from another world—have resulted in the dreamers' transferring them to the printed page as enduring classics of literature, stories and poems that have given inspiration, delight and comfort to millions of readers.

We cannot know to what extent writers have drawn on their dreams for ideas and situations in their stories, but there is no doubt that most of them, either consciously or unconsciously, get help while they are asleep. History does not say whether William Shakespeare dreamed "A Midsummer Night's Dream," but it is a safe guess that the play had something in it of many dreams, for its eerie, haunting quality reminds us of the dream life that we all know.

Robert Louis Stevenson, one of the best loved authors of the past hundred years, dreamed of a struggle between a

16

man's two natures, his baser passions and his better self, and thereupon wrote the stirring novelette, "Dr. Jekyll and Mr. Hyde." It is said that the incidents of the story followed the dream closely.

John Bunyan had a dream that he perpetuated for the world in the immortal allegory "Pilgrim's Progress," which for centuries has been rated as one of the world's great masterpieces.

Samuel Taylor Coleridge dreamed the poem "Kubla Khan," whose beautiful lines beginning, "In Xanadu did Kubla Khan a stately pleasure dome decree," have been learned by uncounted school children, but, fine as the result was in the field of poetry, the dream was induced by a drug.

Such stimulated dreams, in spite of the fact that they have been the cause of such classics as this, as Francis Thompson's "The Hound of Heaven" and De Quincey's "Confessions of an Opium Eater," are doubtful as to their value in the prediction of future events. The effect of a drug on the sleeping mind is a complicated affair, and the combination of the physiological with the psychological is something that in its premonitory values has yet to be figured out. The wild imaginings of drug-inspired dreams, as revealed by De Quincey and others who have written on the subject; the delicate, unearthly fantasies; the horrible, grotesque, yet sometimes delightful and often musical ideas that have been evolved—the significance of these lies outside of a dream book.

There are references throughout all literatures to dreams and their application to life. The Bible is particularly rich in its allusion to dreams and what they mean, and no one who regards Holy Writ with respect can fail to believe in authoritative dream prophecies.

"Hear now my words: If there be a prophet among you, I the Lord will make myself known unto him in a vision, and will speak unto him in a dream." (Numbers XII:6.)

"Your sons and your daughters shall prophesy, your old men shall dream dreams, your young men shall see visions." (Joel II:28.)

One of the most outstanding and best known dreams mentioned in the Bible is that told in Genesis XVIII:10-16 of Jacob and the ladder ascending into Heaven. In these

17

seven short verses are told the dream and its interpretation within it, as follows:

"And Jacob went out from Beersheba, and went toward Haran.

"And he lighted upon a certain place, and tarried there all night, because the sun was set; and he took of the stones of that place, and put them for his pillows, and lay down in that place to sleep.

"And he dreamed, and behold a ladder set up on the earth, and the top of it reached to Heaven: and behold the angels of God ascending and descending on it.

"And, behold, the Lord stood above it, and said, I am the Lord God of Abraham thy father, and the God of Isaac: the land whereon thou liest, to thee will I give it, and to thy seed;

"And thy seed shall be as the dust of the earth, and thou shalt spread abroad to the west, and to the east, and to the north, and to the south: and in thee and in they seed shall all the families of the earth be blessed.

"And, behold, I am with thee, and will keep thee in all places whither thou goest, and will bring thee again into this land; for I will not leave thee, until I have done that which I have spoken to thee of.

"And Jacob awaked out of his sleep, and he said, 'Surely the Lord is in this place; and I knew it not.' "*

The dignity of the interpretation of dreams cannot be questioned except by those who are ignorant of its development through long ages, beginning in the darkest antiquity. There were professional interpreters of dreams among the ancient Babylonians, Assyrians, Arabs and Egyptians—people who had achieved much in the arts and sciences, and who could not by any stretch of the imagination be classed as merely superstitious barbarians.

As early as the second century after the birth of Christ there was a manual on the subject, compiled by Artemidor-

---

*A few of the many other Biblical references to dreams may be found in Genesis XXXVII: 6-9; Genesis XLI: 25-36; Genesis XXXI: 10-16; Judges VII: 13-16; Daniel II: 28; Daniel VII; St. Matthew I: 20; St. Matthew II: 13, 20; and Job XXXIII: 15-16. Those who wish to pursue the subject of dreams through the Bible should consult a Concordance.

us Daldianus, and called *Oneirocritica,* or "The Interpretation of Dreams." Browsing one hot summer afternoon amid volumes relating to the dream world, I turned up a small gray book that proved to be a translation of this same *Oneirocritica* by the ancient Greek soothsayer. It was published in London over a century and a half ago—the exact year was 1800—and at that time it was in its thirty-third edition. No doubt it was one of the best sellers of that day, sixteen long centuries after it was compiled. And, allowing for scientific developments, it is extremely interesting to notice how closely these interpretations resemble those of dream books published through the nineteenth century and later.

It is quite probable that many hundreds of years before Artemidorus Daldianus wrote out his dream interpretations on a parchment scroll, some shaggy soothsayer laboriously chiseled similar information on a slab back in the Stone Age.

By word of mouth, the chiseled word, and the written word, dream meanings have been handed down to us almost since the beginning of time. The centuries that have rolled by, bringing new knowledge in all realms of thought, have added materially to dream lore; but they have also extended belief in the significance of dreams, until today there is a greater interest than ever before by people of high intelligence.

*   *   *

Dreams are intensely personal.

Some of them cannot be told without making the dreamer appear foolish, or cruel, or narrow-minded, or unjust, or lacking in moral sense. Such dreams are not of necessity an index of the dreamer's character—God forbid, for, as an inveterate dreamer, I have covered a great deal of ground! They should be interpreted according to the principal items emphasized in the dreams.

Everybody knows of the peculiar slants that dreams are liable to have. Some of them have neither rhyme nor reason. They are like a motion picture built of haphazard bits from films that are unrelated. Some of them have plots, like a story. Others are funny. A friend of mine, who happens to be bald-headed and a bachelor, told me of dreaming about being a week-end guest at a large country home. In his dream he met a woman of uncertain age who obviously wore a wig. He found himself seated with her in a lawn hammock. They talked in a friendly but impersonal manner until suddenly she became quite confidential, put her hand on his knee, and said:

"Tell me frankly, Mr. Blank, have you had a permanent wave put in your hair?"

So entirely flabbergasted was Mr. Blank that all he could do was to wake up! But he remembered the dream, and he asked me what it meant. I analyzed it as follows:

A humorous dream, as a rule, is a propitious dream— therefore he was off to a good start. *House-party*, in the first place, predicts joyous living in the future. *Wig* is a sign of threatened treachery. *Woman*, if she is disposed to be friendly—and this woman was—cannot be other than a good influence.

I told my friend that his dream was both an excellent prediction and a warning; that if he was on his guard against treachery, he would have good luck and achieve some great desire. He followed my interpretation, turned down what would have proved to be a disastrous investment, and married a woman with whom he is still living happily after several years.

\* \* \*

It is told that a man had the following dream: He was in church. It was a warm Sunday, and during the sermon, which was long and not very interesting, he went to sleep. He dreamed that he was one of the nobles during the French Revolution, and that he was in hiding from the vengeance of the blood-thirsty proletariat.

He heard the roar of the mob and the rattle of the tumbrils as they slithered over the block pavement carrying the hapless victims to the guillotine.

Finally his hiding place at the top of a house was discovered. Brutal men and women dragged him down four flights of stairs to the street. A tumbril was waiting—one of those homely carts that carried Marie Antoinette to her doom.

Roughly he was pushed into it, and through a hissing, shouting mob he was carried to a public square in which there were thousands of lookers-on for the grisly spectacle that was to follow.

He was seized by two burly ruffians, dragged to the ghastly machine of death, and thrust with his neck beneath where the knife would fall.

The word was given—there was a loathsome *swish*, and a quick evil glint of the sun on the blade. . . .

So realistic was the dream that the man, who had a weak heart, died in his sleep!

No doubt you will realize at once that this is a fake dream, for if the man had died in his sleep, no one would ever know what he had dreamed. If he had waked before the knife had severed his head from his body, it would be quite believable, but as it is told it is nothing more than a sample of someone's fertile imagination—a trick to catch the unwary.

A well authenticated dream of an unusual nature was one in which a man *dreamed of waking up*. Another was related by a man who, never having crossed the ocean but having a great desire to do so, has dreamed frequently of being in London. It is a dream which recurs every few months, and gives him much pleasure. In one of these dreams, the reality of being in London was so strong that *in the dream* he said to himself, "This time it is real—it is not a dream!"

You may expect anything in a dream. Witness the following, told me by a young New York playboy:

"I dreamed," he said, "of being at a very gorgeous party at a large estate in Westchester County, New York. Hundreds of guests were present, and all of them were people of culture and interest. There was music for dancing, and there was a room in which refreshments of every kind were served. All of the women were beautiful, but the most beautiful woman of all was a Russian dancer whose name I never learned.

"For some reason this lovely dancer fell for me like a ton of bricks, and we were together all the evening. Then, as the party broke up, there was a fading of the picture until I found myself in bed with this most glamourous of women. And, believe it or not, *I immediately turned over toward the wall and went to sleep!"*

Dreams of embarrassment are common, and they cover situations of many kinds. One of the most usual is the dream of finding oneself in a public place or at a large formal gathering either absolutely naked or clothed only in scanty undergarments.

Folk whose honesty has never been open to question will dream of being caught at shoplifting or some other form of thievery. Others of the utmost modesty will suffer in their dreams from being seen in the performance of intimately personal actions.

I recall a dream of my own, of an embarrassing nature, wherein I was at a fair of some sort and happened to meet two women, both of whom I had known for many years. They did not know each other, so the natural thing was for me to introduce them. I began to do so, and had to stop because I could not remember either of their names. An end was put to my embarrassment only by my waking up, and I dare say that anyone seeing me at that time would have noticed that my ears were red.

Over and above their value as predictions of future events is the fascination of adventure in dreams. Such dreams often come with a startling and satisfying reality. A person whose waking life may be humdrum will sometimes find release in dreams by piloting a huge airplane, driving a locomotive, taming a snarling lion, stopping a runaway horse, "waving the five fingers of scorn" at a bill collector, or giving a "Bronx cheer" to his mother-in-law. It is not beyond the bounds of possibility that a mouse dreams of slapping a cat in the face!

We have played the piano like a Paderewski, danced like a Pavlova, performed surgical operations that the Doctors Mayo would not dare attempt, written poems in Sanskrit, and driven a motor car across the Rocky Mountains at a hundred miles an hour. All this is very exhilarating at the time, and I recommend getting all the fun possible out of dreaming; but nevertheless, dreams, enjoyable or not, should be interpreted strictly by the book.

Occasionally dreams will be fulfilled almost to the letter, as in Lincoln's premonitory dream of his death. Another evidence of this is the following Associated Press dispatch dated March 19, 1937, published in many metropolitan and other newspapers, wherein it is told how a tragic dream came true:

"New London, Texas.—Two nights ago George M. Davidson, oil field driller and wartime hero, visualized tragedy in a dream.

"Before breakfast yesterday he told members of his crew about the dream. They warned it was an ill omen to relate dream tragedies before the morning meal.

"Ten hours later he stumbled into an Overton morgue and identified three bodies as those of his two daughters and a son—Anna Laura, 11, Helen, 13, and Joe Wheeler, 15."

There are on record hundreds of well authenticated cases of similar import. They are by no means all of a tragic character. Many a dream that comes true means life long happiness for the dreamer.

\*　\*　\*

Authorities do not always agree in their interpretations of dreams. This is no more strange than that doctors do not agree in every diagnosis of disease. If you delve into some of the ancient interpreters, you will find, for instance, that Astrampsychus says that to dream of cutting the hair signifies losses in business, while one of the comparatively modern dream books, published some 1500 years later, says that cutting the hair shows that you will be generous to a friend. It is just possible, however, that both authorities are right, for no one can deny that being generous to a friend—he might be a creditor, in fact—could cause losses in business.

The use of a dream book requires intelligence and discretion. What your dreams mean, and what they predict, depends on more than one factor. If you dream of *cheese,* for instance, you must take the accompanying circumstances into consideration.

You may *eat* cheese
    *see* cheese
    *make* cheese
    *smell* cheese

This may be in *a store*
     *your home*
     *a restaurant*
     *on a picnic*
     or elsewhere

The cheese may be *domestic*
      *foreign*
      *in curious shape*
      *in packages*

Each circumstance is capable of analysis. In eating cheese, for example, there are the matters of flavor and consistency; and in smelling cheese there is a wide range of possibilities, from agreeable to ill smelling. The condition of the cheese is also a factor—dry, moist, hard, soft, crumbly, fresh or moldy.

In seeking the meaning of your dream, in other words, do not jump at conclusions. Study the references carefully and do not overlook any conditions that might alter an interpretation and upset a prophecy. Remember that certain words have two or more meanings, according to the manner in which they are used. It is much the same with dreams—the context, or what is included with them has a distinct bearing on the interpretation.

Your own intelligence in working out the interpretations will contribute to their accuracy.

# ANCIENT INTERPRETATIONS OF DREAMS

# CHAPTER II

Over a period of one thousand years or more there have been interpretations of dreams that people have had. On these interpretations have been built the dream books of today. Changes in modes of living and advances in science have occurred that have made considerable differences in the manner of interpreting dreams, but many of the solutions of sleeping thoughts have remained the same.

Following are some of the interpretations that have come down through the ages.

## THE ONEIROCRITICON OF ASTRAMPSYCHUS

"To talk in dreams is a sign of their truth.
To move slowly denotes unfortunate journey.
It is good to fly, for it is the sign of an honourable deed.
Laughter in sleep presages difficult circumstances.
To weep in sleep is a sign of the utmost joy.
To eat with enemies indicates a reconciliation.
To be dead in dreams announces freedom from anxiety.
An offensive odour signifies annoyance.
If anyone offer incense to you, it portends affliction.
If you seem to be an old man, you will attain to honour.
To run in dreams shows the stability of your circumstances.
To wash the hands denotes the release from anxieties.
To clean the feet denotes the release from anxieties.
To clean the body denotes the release from anxieties.
To cut the hair signifies losses in business.
To lose the hair heralds great danger.
To see white meats is exceedingly advantageous.
To see black meats forebodes evil to one's children.
To embrace your mother is to have a lucky dream.

To embrace one's best beloved is very fortunate.

All embraces bring about protracted labours.

To kiss or to love excites the long-continued opposition of one's enemies.

To have broad feet is a sign of misfortune.

The amputation of the feet is a bar to a contemplated journey.

The burning of the body indicates a very evil reputation.

Gladness of mind shows that you will live abroad.

For a blind man to see is the best omen possible.

To wear a white robe is an excellent omen.

To wear a black one is a mournful spectacle.

To wear a purple robe threatens a long disease.

To wear a red one promises an honourable action.

To wear the pall of kings is the solution of our expectations.

The tearing of a garment is relief from the burden of anxieties.

A severed girdle speedily cuts short a journey.

To behold the stars forebodes much good to men.

Thunder-peals in dreams are the words of messengers.

To see lights indicates guidance in affairs.

The sight of snow figures the hostilities of enemies.

The sight of the dead indicates the ruin of affairs.

The sight of withered trees declares the uselessness of labours.

Pearls denote a torrent of tears.

Milk confounds the politics of enemies.

Milk is the sign of peaceful circumstances.

Clay or mud symbolizes the sordid avarice of the disposition.

A pellucid fountain dispels the distresses of the mind.

Wine poured from the vessels soothes the distresses of the mind.

Musty wine announces many difficulties.

To mix different wines is to invite serious quarrels.

Water gushing up from below is a sign of enemies.

To drain a cup of clear water is a lucky token.

The pouring out of rivers dissipates the joy of enemies.

To stand in the assemblies brings with it a crime.

Sitting naked signifies loss of property.

Sitting on a dunghill signifies disastrous circumstances.

Sitting upon a stone, you may conceive great expectations.

Sitting on a wall indicates coming prosperity.

To embark on a lake is a sign of evil.

To walk over live coals signifies loss from one's enemies.

To walk over potsherds signifies loss of one's enemies.

To creep up a mountain signifies the difficulty of business.

To tread upon serpents is to blunt the sharp attacks of foes.

If you sail over mud, look out for mental disquiet.

The falling from a precipice is an evil omen.

The eating of sweets portends disagreeable circumstances.

To swallow bunches of grapes indicates a deluge of rain.

To feed on lettuces is a sign of disease of the body.

To drink muddy water foretells disease of the body.

If you are governing children, expect a coming danger.

To hold a bull is to be disappointed of one's hopes.

If anyone holds goods, let him fear the attacks of his enemies.

A broken staff portends an unhappy death.

To catch falcons indicates the fulfilment of your utmost desires.

To hold keys signifies the settlement of affairs.

To hold a twig foreshadows a prosecution.

To seize a sword is the sign of a contest.

To handle threads is a presage of troublesome circumstances.

To hold a sparrow, struggling to escape, forebodes mischief.

To grasp a pillar is to expect the Divine favour.

To shiver a sword signifies the crushing of one's foes.

The escape of a hawk from the hand is disastrous to those in power.

To hold gold is a warning to leave one's project undone.

To hold eggs, or to eat eggs, symbolizes vexation.

To behold oxen in dreams is of evil tendency.

To see black mares is a thoroughly bad sign.

The sight of white horses is a vision of angels.

To see lions announces the contentions of one's enemies.

The sight of doves is the introduction of injury.

To see a colt running denotes something mysterious.

The barking of a dog portends the detriment of one's enemies.

A gaping wolf signifies nonsensical discourse.

The sight of a mouse bespeaks propitious circumstances.
Dead oxen signify times of famine.
The sight of wasps marks injuries to one's foes.
The sight of a hare portends an unlucky journey.
If you see oil, you will escape every misfortune.
To see the ocean calm is favourable.
The noise of the sea stands for the throng of business.
To swim in the sea forebodes bitter sorrows.
To dream in the daytime of swimming in the sea is good.
The eating of figs signifies nonsensical discourse."

## INTERPRETATIONS FROM ARTEMIDORUS AND OTHERS

### A

ACQUAINTANCE. To dream that you fight with them signifies distraction, especially if the person so dreaming be sick.

ADULTERY. For persons to dream they have committed it, shows that they shall meet with great contentions and debates; but to dream they have resisted the temptation to it shows victory over their enemies, and that they shall escape great dangers.

ADVERSARY. To dream that you receive obstructions from him, shows that you shall dispatch your business speedily.

AIR. To dream that you see it clear and serene, shows you to be esteemed and beloved by all people, and that those who are your enemies and envy you shall be reconciled to you. It also denotes the discovery of lost goods, or things that have been stolen. If the person so dreaming be at law, it shows he shall overthrow his adversary; and if he designs a voyage or journey, it shows he shall be successful therein. And, in short, all good things are denoted by a clear and serene *Air*. But to dream the *Air* is cloudy, dark, and troubled, denotes to the dreamer sadness, grief, sickness, melancholy, loss of goods, hindrance of business, and is in all things the reverse of dreaming what we have before mentioned of a clear and serene air. But for a man to dream that the air is very calm, and without winds and storms, denotes his life to be peaceable, and his manners good, and that he shall be acceptable to all company; and that whatever business, journeys by land, or voyages by sea, he undertakes shall prosper and succeed according to his wishes. And yet there are some authors who are of opinion that a serene air betokens great pain, and that to dream the air is cloudy, shows dispatch of business. To dream of being raised from the earth and flying in the air, shows a person shall obtain praise and honor, according to the height that he dreams he flies above the earth: if high, the more praise; if low, the less.

ALMONDS. To dream one sees or eats almonds signifies difficulty and trouble.

ALMS. To dream they are begged of you, and you deny to give them, shows want and misery to the dreamer; but to dream that you give them freely, is a sign of great joy, and long life to the dreamer or some particular friend of his.

ALTAR. To dream that you uncover or discover an altar betokens joy and gladness.

ANGEL. To dream you see an angel or angels is very good, and to dream that you yourself are one is much better. But to speak with or call upon them is of evil signification. Yet if in secret they seem to declare something unknown, and which you do not understand or know, it denotes your becoming acquainted with persons of the first quality. And to dream that you see an angel fly over you or your house, signifies joy, consolation, benediction, and good news, and shows increase of honor and authority.

ANGLING. To dream that you are angling betokens much affliction and trouble in seeking for something you desire to get.

**APES.** To dream you have seen, or had anything to do with them, signifies malicious, weak, strange, and secret enemies; also malefactors and deceivers.

## B

**BACK.** To dream you see your back, betokens some unhappiness, for the back and all the hinder parts signify old-age; therefore, as a man thinks his hinder parts to be, so shall he be in his age. To dream a man's back is broken, hurt, or disfigured, shows his enemies will get the better of him, and that he will be scoffed at by all persons. To dream of the backbone signifies health and joy, and domestic comfort and prosperity.

**BAGPIPES.** To dream that you play upon bagpipes signifies trouble, contention, and being overthrown at law.

**BARLEY-BREAD.** To dream of eating barley-bread signifies health and content.

**BASILISK.** When you dream of woman that she is delivered of a basilisk instead of a child, it is a bad hieroglyphic, and betokens no good to the dreamer; and he ought heartily to recommend himself to the Divine Being, that he would preserve him, and avert those misfortunes that threaten him. And if it be a woman that has such a dream, many authors—Anselmus Julianus in particular, who is an author to whom great regard ought to be had—affirm that she shall have very good success and comfort, shall be rich and generally beloved, and shall prosper in all her undertakings.

**BEARD.** To dream you have a beard long, thick and unhandsome, is of a good signification to an orator, or an ambassador, lawyer, philospher, or any who desires to speak well, or to learn arts and sciences. If one dreams he hath a comely beard, it shows he shall be pleasant in his discourse, find out the intricacies of the matter proposed, and prosper in his undertakings. If a maid dreams that she hath a beard, she will be speedily matched to her content. If she be a married woman, such a dream threatens her with the loss of her husband, or that she shall be separated from him, and constrained to govern her house singly as if she were a man. If it be a woman with child that so dreams, it shows she shall have a son. If a widow woman dreams she hath a beard, she shall have a husband who shall be kind and bountiful. If she be at law it shows she shall persevere in her opinion; and, bearing a high mind, regard her honor, and vindicate it as if she were a man. To a young child this dream is death; but to him who is now in his youth, beginning to have a beard, it is a sign he shall rise by himself, and put himself forward, of what estate soever he be. If one dreams that he hath lost his beard, or that somebody hath pulled it up by the roots or shaved it, it denotes loss of relations, estates, and honor. To dream that one hath a great heart, in a young man betokeneth wisdom; in an old man length of years; but in a woman that she shall be a furious vixen, and wear the breeches.

BEES. To dream of bees is good and bad: good, if they sting not; but bad, if they sting the party dreaming, for then they signify enemies. And therefore to dream that bees fly about your ears, shows your being beset with many enemies; but if you beat them off without being stung by them, it is a sign of victory and of your overcoming them. To dream of seeing bees, signifies profit to country people, and trouble to the rich; yet to dream that they make their honey in any part of a house or tenement, signifies to the occupier dignity, eloquence, and good success in business. But to dream you are stung by a bee signifies vexation and trouble. To take bees signifies profit and gain. To dream of bees is good to ploughmen, and to such as thereby get profit. To others they signify trouble by reason of the noise they make; and wounds by reason of their sting, and sickness by reason of their honey and wax.

BELLS. To dream that one hears ringing of bells, if of a sanguine complexion, brings him good news; but to others it shows alarms, murmurings, disturbances, and commotions among citizens. To dream one plays tunes on small bells signifies discord and disunion between subjects and servants. To dream you pull a rope of the bell, and see a spirit keep it from ringing, shows trouble and molestation; and if it be a parson that is the dreamer, it shows he shall meet with some disturbance in his preaching.

BITTERN. To dream of a Bittern, which is a night bird, is a bad omen.

BLEEDING. To dream of bleeding at the nose signifies loss of goods, and decay of riches to those who are phlegmatic and melancholy; but to the choleric and sanguine, it signifies health and joy.

BOOTS. To dream that one is well booted or hath good boots on, signifies honor and profit by servants.

BROW. To dream that you have a brow of brass, copper, marble, or iron, signifies irreconcilable hatred against your enemies.

BURIED. For a man to dream that he is buried and interred, signifies he shall have as much wealth as he hath earth laid over him.

## C

CARDS. To dream one plays at cards or dice, signifies deceit and craft, and that he is in danger of losing his estate by some wicked person. And yet playing at cards, tables, or any other game in a dream, shows the party shall be very fortunate, if the tables allude to love; for love is the table, fancy the point that stands open, and he that dreams of table-playing shall be a great gamester as well with Joan as my lady.

CAT. If anyone dreams that he hath encountered a cat or killed one, he will commit a thief to prison and prosecute him to the death; for the cat signifies a common thief. If he dreams that he eats cat's flesh, he will have the goods of the thief that robbed him: if he dream he hath the skin, then he will have all the thief's goods. If anyone dreams he fought with a cat that scratched him sorely, that denotes some sickness or affliction. If any shall dream that a woman was delivered of a cat, instead of a well-shaped child, it is a bad hieroglyphic, and betokens no good to the dreamer. Also the cat signifies a person of loose morals.

CATERPILLARS. To dream you see caterpillars signifies ill-luck and misfortunes from secret enemies.

CHEESE. To dream you eat cheese signifies profit and gain.

CHICKENS. To dream of a hen and her chickens signifies loss and damage.

CLAVICORD. To dream one plays, or sees another play upon a clavicord, shows the death of relations or funeral obsequies.

COALPITS. To dream of being in the bottom of coalpits signifies matching with a widow; for he that marries her must be a continual drudge, and yet shall never sound the depth of her policies.

COMEDY. To dream you see a comedy, farce, or some other recreation, signifies good success in business.

COMMAND. To dream you command one signifies trouble; to dream you see one command signifies anger and authority.

CONFECTIONS. To dream that one makes confections and sweetmeats betokens pleasure and profit.

CORNS. For a man to dream that his flesh is full of corns, shows he will grow rich proportionably to the corns.

COUNTENANCE. To dream you see a comely countenance, unlike your own, signifies honor.

CROWN. To dream of having a crown of gold on your head signifies the friendship of your liege; and the dreamer will be honored by many persons, and will have many gifts.

# D

DAIRY. To dream of being in a dairy, showeth the dreamer to be of a milk-sop nature.

DEAD-FOLKS. To dream of talking with dead-folks is a good, auspicious dream, and signifies a boldness of courage, and a very clear conscience.

DEER. To dream of hunting deer signifies going to law or to the wars, or falling out with your best friend upon a slight occasion.

DEVIL. To dream that one has seen the devil, and that he is tormented, or otherwise much terrified, signifies that the dreamer is in danger of being checked and punished by his sovereign prince, or some magistrate. And quite contrarily, if he dreams he strikes the devil, or some person he believes to be possessed, and fancies he overcomes him, it is a sign he that dreams thus shall overcome his enemies with glory and satisfaction. If any dream that he sees the devil, it is a very bad sign, for such a vision cannot bring along with it any good tidings; to the sick it foretells death, and to the healthful it signifies melancholy, anger, tumults, and violent sickness. If any dream the devil speaks to him, it signifies temptation, deceit, treachery, despair, and sometimes the ruin and death of him that dreams. To dream that one is carried away by the devil, is a worse dream; and yet no dream delights the dreamer so much as this, for being awakened he is ravished with joy that he is freed from so great an evil; for which he ought to return thanks to God, and beg of him that he would be pleased to send him his good angel to guard him, and fight against that wicked spirit which stands always sentinel to surprise us. To dream you see the devil as he is drawn by painters, and poets, viz. black and hideous, with horns, claws, and a great tail, signifies torment and despair. To dream you see yourself with the devil, signifies gain.

**DIVINE SERVICE.** To dream you go to Divine service, signifies honor and joy.

**DRAGONS.** To dream you see a dragon, is a sign that you shall see some great lord your master, or a magistrate; it signifies also riches and treasure.

**DRINK.** To drink warm water is bad; to drink muddy water is very bad; to drink clear water is a good sign; to drink thick wine is very good; to drink white wine signifies health; to drink milk is an exceedingly good sign; to drink vinegar signifies discomfort.

**DRUNKARDS.** To dream one is drunk, is very bad for all, for it signifieth great folly. It is only good to such as are in fear; for drunkards doubt or fear nothing. To dream one is drunk is increase of estate, and recovery of health; but when one dreams he is drunk, without drinking any wine, it is an ill omen, and he runs the hazard of being disgraced by some bad action, and of being punished by law. If a man dreams he is drunk with sack, muscatel, or some other sweet and pleasant drink, it is a sign he will be beloved by some great lords, and grow rich thereby. If a man dreams he is drunk and vomits, he will run the hazard of losing his estate by the violence of his prince, who will force him to an account of his means ill-gotten; or if he be a gamester, he will lose all he hath formerly won. If anyone dreams that being drunk, he is very much pained at heart and in his viscera, it shows that his domestics or servants will rob him of his money, or destroy his fortune without his knowledge. If a man dreams he is drunk with pure water, he will boast causelessly of his wealth, and vaunt of another person's strength.

# E

**EAGLE.** To dream that an eagle is seen in some high place, is a good sign to those that undertake some weighty business, and especially to soldiers. If one dream that an eagle lights upon his head, it signifies death to the dreamer; and the same if he dreams that he is carried into the air by an eagle. If a woman dreams that she brings forth an eagle, it portends that the child she goes withal will be a great person, and have many persons under his command. If one dreams that he sees a dead eagle, it signifies death to great peers, and profit to the poor. To see an eagle flying over a stone or a tree, or in a high place, is good for those which would undertake business; but to those who are in fear, it is evil; also it signifies the return of him that is in a far country. And if his flight be far, and at ease and pleasure, it is good and signifieth that the business shall have an end, but not so soon. An eagle flying strongly, and falling upon the head of him that dreameth, certainly signifies to kings, princes, and mighty and rich personages, death; but to the poor it is good, for they shall be welcome and received of all rich men, from whom they shall receive great profit. Oftentimes it causeth changing one's country, and going to another nation. The eagle threatening, signifieth the threatening of some great personage. But to dream of his being gentle, or giving anything, or to dream that he spake, hath been found a good dream by experience. To see an eagle that is dead is good for a servant and him that is in fear, for it denotes the death of the master and threatener; and unto others it shows that a stop shall be put to their affairs, for a dead eagle can do nothing.

**EARTHWORMS.** To dream of earthworms signifies secret enemies that endeavor to ruin and destroy us; and that this shall be effected by misers and covetous persons, who are the mere worms of the earth.

**EAT.** To dream of eating human flesh signifies labor and distress; to eat lard or salt signifies murmuring; to eat cheese signifies gain and profit; to eat apples signifies anger.

EGGS. To dream of eggs signifies gain and profit, especially to physicians, painters, and to those which sell and trade with them. To others it is good to have little store of them; for plenty of them signifies care, pain, noise, and lawsuits. To dream you see broken eggs is a very ill sign, and signifies loss to the party dreaming.

EVIL SPIRITS. To dream that evil spirits obstruct your doing good under the show of devotion, shows you shall be obstructed in your affairs by a hypocrite, who shall be a priest. And if you dream that you see hideous physiognomies, things more than vulgar shall be revealed to you.

EYEBROWS. To dream the eyebrows are hairy and of a good grace, is good to all, especially to women; but the eyebrows naked, and without hair, signifieth to all ill-success in business, and to some single combats and grief. If anyone dreams his eyebrows are more comely and large than they used to be, it is a sign that he will be honored and esteemed by all persons, and that he will prosper in courtship and grow rich.

## F

FACE. To dream you see a fresh, taking, smiling face and countenance, is a sign of friendship and joy. To dream you see a meager, pale face, is a sign of trouble, poverty, and death. To dream one washes his face denotes repentance for sin; a black face signifies long life.

FALCON. To dream a man carries a falcon upon his fist and walks with it, signifies honor. Also the falcon and the kite signify thieves and robbers.

FIELDS. To dream of fields and pleasant places, shows to a man that he will marry a discreet, chaste, and beautiful wife, and that she will bear him very handsome children.

And to a woman it betokens a loving and prudent husband, by whom she shall have beautiful children.

FIGS. To dream that you see figs in season, is a good dream, and signifies joy and pleasure; but out of season, the contrary.

FILBERTS. To dream of filberts is trouble and anger.

FIREBRANDS. To dream you hold firebrands and torches by night is good, especially to young folk, to whom it often signifieth love with pleasure and effect. But to see another hold a firebrand, is ill to those that would be secret.

FIRE FROM HEAVEN.
When thou dreamest fire from Heaven is sent,
Some extraordinary thing is meant;
A king or prince that often dreameth so
Will in his country find both war and woe.

FLIES. To dream you see a swarm of flies signifies enemies and unreasonable persons that will scandalize you. To dream that you shut in flies, and that you kill them, is good to all except to countrymen and ploughmen.

FOOLS. For a man to dream that he is a fool is good to him who would undertake any business; for fools and madmen do that which comes into their brain. It is good also for marshals and sheriffs, who would have authority over the people; for they shall have great honor and repute. It is also good for those who would govern and teach children; for children do willingly follow fools. It is also good for the poor, for they shall have goods; for fools catch on all sides and all hands. To the sick it is health, for folly makes men go and come, not sleep and rest.

FOWLING. For a man to dream he goes fowling with his gun, and kills good store of game, shows he shall reap great advantage by his calling, and according to the game he takes or kills so shall his profit be in his calling; if he kills much game, his profit shall be great, but if little, the less; and the signification is the same if you dream of fishing.

FRUIT. To dream of fruit has a different interpretation, according to what the fruit is. Apples show long life and success; a boy to a woman with child; cheerfulness in your sweetheart, and riches in trade. Cherries indicate disappointment in love, and vexation in the married state.

FROGS. To dream of frogs is good for them that live upon the commons. "I knew a man," says Artemidorus, "who dreamed that he beat with his fist, and the knuckles or joints of his fingers, upon frogs, and it so happened that his master gave him authority over all the affairs of his house; so that one must think that the pond represents the house, the frogs the inhabitants, and the striking of his fingers the commandment." But as to frogs in general, they signify flatterers, indifferent and ignorant babblers, abusers, and praters.

FUNERALS. To dream that one goes to the funeral and interment of any of his relations or friends, or of some great lord, is a good sign to the dreamer, who is betokened thereby to get an estate by means of his relations, or else marry a fortune to his content.

# G

GARDEN. To dream of walking in a garden and gathering here and there a flower, shows a person to be much given to pride and arrogancy, and to have high thoughts of him or herself. To dream of seeing fair gardens shows a man will marry a chaste and beautiful wife, for gardens are strictly enclosed.

GEESE. To dream you hear the cackling of geese signifies profit, assurance, and dispatch of business.

41

**GELDING.** To dream you see a gelding signifies accusation.

**GIBBERISH.** For a man to dream he hears gibberish shows he shall have to do with gypsies, rogues, and common beggars.

**GLEBE.** To dream a man has much glebe-land adjoining to his house is good for a clergyman, for it shows he shall suddenly obtain a good benefice.

**GLOVES.** To dream one has gloves on his hands signifies honor and safety.

**GOATS.** Though, according to Artemidorus, to dream of goats signifies no good, but is worst of all to navigators: yet, according to other authors, to dream of she-goats is a sign of wealth and plenty.

**GOD.** To dream that we worship God, and call upon Him, gives to the soul the highest joy; and to dream that we receive pure gifts from Him is a good dream, and shows great health to those that dream so; but to dream of receiving impure gifts from Him signifies disease, misery, and woe.

**GOLD.** To dream your clothes are embroidered with gold signifies joy and honor. If a man dreams that he gathers up gold and silver, that signifies deceit and loss. If anyone dreams that his pockets are full of gold, it betokeneth that he shall receive but little money. To dream one hath a crown of gold upon his head signifies favor with his sovereign, and that he shall be honored and feared by many. For a man to dream that he hath found gold and cannot tell where to hide it, or that he is afraid to be taken with it, shows he will have a wife who shall rob his purse and take away all his money while he is asleep.

**GOOD.** To dream that we do good to anyone, signifies jollity and pleasure; and to dream that others do us good, is profit and gain.

**GRAPES.** To dream of eating grapes at any time signifies cheerfulness and profit. To tread grapes signifies the overthrow of enemies. To gather white grapes signifies gain, but to dream of gathering black grapes signifies damage.

**GRAVE.** If a man dreams that he is put into a grave and buried, it presageth he will die in a mean condition; yet some believe (grounded on experience) that to dream that one is dead and buried signifieth he that hath such a dream shall recover an estate according to the quantity of earth that is laid upon him.

# H

**HAIL.** To dream of hail signifies sorrow and trouble, and sometimes that the most hidden secrets shall be revealed and made known. To dream of great and long-continued hail, attended with tempest and thunder, signifies afflictions, troubles, dangers, losses, and perils; though to the poorer sort such dreams signify repose, for during storms they are shut up and at rest.

**HANGING OR HANGED.** If anyone dreams that by sentence or judgment he was condemned to be hanged, and dreams also that the sentence was really executed, he will be dignified according to the height of the gibbet or tree whereon he was hanged. But if the dreamer be sick or afflicted, he will be freed from his disease, and in the end have joy and contentment. If anyone dreams he condemned another to be hanged, that signifies he will be angry with him whom he imagined he condemned, but in a small time after he will place him in honor and dignity, which he will abuse. According to the interpretations of the Persians and the Egyptians, he that dreams he is hanged by sentence of law, will be rich, honored, and respected. If anyone dreams that he has eaten the flesh of a man hanged, he will be enriched by some person, but it will be by some foul practice and some secret crime. If anyone dreams that, being about to be hanged, he was

43

delivered, and came down to the bottom of the gibbet, that person will lose his estate and dignity.

HARPIES. To dream you see harpies, which are infernal creatures, half women and half serpents, or else furies, such as the poets feign them to be, signifies tribulation and pains occasioned by envious persons, and such as seek our ruin, shame, or death, by mischief and treachery.

HART. If anyone dreams he killed a hart, and that he had the head and skin, it signifies that he will inherit the estate of some old man, or that he will overcome fugitive, deceitful, timorous, and irresolute enemies. To see a hart running, shows great wealth got by subtlety.

HAT. To dream that your hat is broken, or fallen off, means damage and dishonor.

HEAVEN. To dream of heaven, and that you ascend up thither, signifies grandeur and glory.

HELL. A dream that one sees hell as it is described, and that he hears the damned souls groan and complain through the extremity of their torments, is an advertisement that God sends to the dreamer to the end that he may throw himself upon God's mercy. If anyone dreams he sees the damned plunged in the fire and flames of hell, and that they suffer great torture, it signifies sadness, repentance, and a melancholic distemper. To dream of descending into hell, and returning thence, to those that are great and rich signifies misfortune; but it is a good sign to the poor and weak.

HOLY VIRGIN. To dream that one speaks to the Holy Virgin signifies consolation, recovery of health, and all good fortune.

HUNGER. To dream one is extraordinarily hungry, and that his appetite craves sustenance, shows that he will be ingenious, laborious, and eager in getting an estate, and that he will grow rich in proportion to the greatness of his hunger.

HYDRA. To dream you see a serpent, or seven-headed hydra, signifies sin and temptation.

HYSSOP. To dream that you smell hyssop signifies labor, trouble, sickness, and weakness. From this rule physicians only are to be excepted, to whom such dreams are propitious.

# I

IDIOT. If anyone dreams that he is turned idiot, and mad, and is guilty of public extravagancies, he shall be long-lived, a favorite with his prince, and shall gain pleasure and profit by the people.

INFERNAL THINGS. If anyone dreams that he sees the devil, or any other infernal spirit or representation, it is a very bad dream, bringing along with it to them that are sick, death; and to the healthful, melancholy, anger, tumults, and violent sickness.

IRON. For one to dream that he sees himself hurt with iron signifies that he shall receive some damage. To dream that one trades with a stranger in iron, signifies to the dreamer losses and misfortune.

# J

JAWS. The jaws represent cellars, shops, and other things used to keep merchandise or other goods, so that if we dream our jaws suffer any harm, we may expect some loss in the things represented by them.

JOLLITY. To dream of joy and festivals by night is good for such as would marry, or make marriages, and for such as seek company and affinity. To the poor it is a sign of good; to the sad and fearful an end of heaviness and fear, for none spend the night in dancing, good cheer, and mirth, but those that are joyful. To persons of evil morals it is the revelation of their deeds; to the rich and wealthy, trouble and divulgation.

# K

KEYS. To dream that you lose your keys signifies anger. To dream you have a bunch of keys, and that you give them to those that desire them of you, shows great good to poor captives, for it implies that shortly they shall gain their liberty. A key seen in a dream, to him who would marry signifieth a good and handsome wife, and a good housekeeper. It is cross to a traveler, for it signifieth he shall be put back and hindered and not received. It is good for such as would take in hand other men's business.

KILL. To dream you kill a man signifies assuredness of business; to dream you kill your father, is a bad sign; to dream you are killed, denotes loss to him who has killed you.

KITE. To dream of seeing a kite, shows you shall be in danger of robbers.

.KNAVE. For a man to dream that himself is a knave, is a sign that he shall grow rich; but for a man to dream that he has to do, or is connected with knaves, shows he shall have many lawsuits.

KNIVES. For a man to dream that he sees knives, shows he shall be engaged with some of his friends and acquaintance in a very hot contest and quarrel; but that after a few hot words all shall be pacified, and they shall be good friends again.

# L

LABOR. To dream that a woman is in labor, and that she brings forth a child that is dead, or else none at all, though she has suffered much pain and anguish in her labor, shows that the party so dreaming shall labor much for that which they shall never bring to pass. But though her labor be hard, if the dream is to the effect that she brings forth a living child, it shows that the party so dreaming shall effect their business, though not without great toil and trouble.

LADDER. The ladder is a sign of traveling; the steps are advancement: but some say they are danger. To dream that you ascend a ladder, signifies honor; but to dream that you descend a ladder betokeneth damage.

LANTERN. He that dreams he sees a lantern with a light in it extinguished or darkened—that signifies unto him sadness, sickness, and poverty.

LAW. As to matters of law, to him that dreams of places of pleading, judges, attorneys, proctors, or other persons concerned in the law, it signifies trouble, anger, expense, and revealing of secrets. And if the sick man dreams he obtains his suit, he shall come to better estate; but if otherwise, he shall die. And if he which is at law dreams that he sits in the judge's seat, he shall not be overthrown, but rather his adversary. A physician seen in a dream by him who is at law, signifies the same with attorneys and proctors.

LEAPING. To dream of leaping demonstrates an active and merry disposition.

LEEKS. To dream of leeks signifies a discovery of secret and domestic jars.

LENTILS. To dream of lentils signifies corruption.

LIGHT. He that dreams he is in a ship, and sees a clear light afar off, shall be assured of a fair wind, and receive no damage by tempests, but arrive happily at his desired haven. When one dreams that he holds a burning light in his hands in the night, it is a good sight, and chiefly to those who are young; for it signifies that they shall prosper in love, accomplish their designs, overcome their enemies, and gain honor and goodwill from all persons. To dream you see a burning light in the hands of another, signifies that the mischief done will be discovered, and the party punished.

LINEN. To dream you are dressed in clean linen, denotes that you will shortly receive some glad tidings; if it is dirty, then it denotes poverty, a prison, and disappointment in love, with the loss of something valuable.

LION. To dream that you see a lion signifies you shall discourse with the king or some great captain, or other valiant warrior. If any dreams he combats with a lion, it signifies a quarrel, and that he shall engage with some resolute adversary; and if he dreamed he came off victorious, it shall certainly be so. If anyone dreams that he hath found the skin, liver, or marrow of a lion—if he that dreamt it be a king, he will find the treasure of his enemies; if he be a vulgar person, he will suddenly grow rich. The Queen Olympias, being big with Alexander the Great, dreamed that King Philip, her husband, had sealed up her womb with a seal engraven with a lion, which did prognosticate the valor, magnanimity, and conquests of the said Alexander. The lioness signifies the same as the lion, only less good and less hurt, and that not by men but by women. "I have also known by a dream of a lioness tearing or biting," says Artemidorus, "that rich personages have fallen into crimes and accusations."

LIZARDS. To dream that a man sees a lizard signifies ill luck, and misfortune by secret enemies.

LOGS. To dream that one is cleaving of logs is a sign that strangers shall come to the house of the party dreaming, or that he is an arrant cotquean.

LOOKING OR LOOKING-GLASS. To dream of looking down from high places, or out of windows, or being in a high garret, shows an ambitious mind, curious desires, wandering imagination, and confused thoughts. To dream of looking in a glass, in married folks, betokens children; in young folks, sweethearts. For as the glass does represent their likeness, so does love show them their like in affection. For a young woman to dream that she looks in a glass and there sees her own face, esteeming it to be very handsome, shows her to have a great opinion of her own beauty. Also for one to dream that he sees himself in the water is death to the dreamer, or to some familiar friend of his.

**LORD.** To dream you discourse with a great lord, or that you go into any place with him, signifies honor.

**LOST AND LOSING.** For a woman to dream she has lost her wedding-ring, signifies she has but small love for her husband; but if she dreams she has found it again, it is a sign her love is not wholly lost. And if a man dream of losing his shoes, and then his feet are bare, if he be of a sanguine complexion, it signifies he shall meet with reproaches, especially if he dreams it in the first day of the new moon.

## M

**MACE.** To dream of mace (the spice so called) is very good, because mace comforts the heart.

**MACE BEARER.** To dream that one carries or bears the mace before the king or chief governor, shows that the dreamer is to arrive at great honor in a little time.

**MALLOWS.** To dream of eating mallows signifies exemption from trouble and dispatch of business, because this herb renders the body soluble.

**MANURE.** To dream that a man manures or cultivates earth, signifies melancholy to those that are not of such a condition; but to laborers it signifies gain and a good crop.

49

**MARE.** If any man dreams he sees a young, generous mare come into his house, well harnessed, it is a sign that he is to be suddenly married to a beautiful, young, and rich gentlewoman, that will be delightful and comfortable to him. If it be an ill-shapen mare, without saddle, that denotes a maid-servant who will be disadvantageous to him.

**MARROW.** If anyone dreams he hath found the marrow of a horned beast, it denotes that the party so dreaming shall enjoy the goods and estate of some person of quality, who shall make him his heir; for the horns signify dignity and sovereignty, and therefore in dreams horns are put to represent crowns.

**MARRY.** To dream that you marry signifies damage, sickness, melancholy, and sometimes death. If a sick person so dream, it is an evident token of death.

**MASON.** To dream you build a house, or play the mason, signifies molestation, loss, sickness, or death, and is a very unhappy dream.

**MEAT.** To dream you see the meat you nave already eaten, signifies loss and damage to the dreamer.

**MIDWIFE.** To dream you see a midwife is a revealing of secrets, and signifies hurt. It is death to the sick, for she always pulleth out that which is contained from her which containeth it, and layeth it on the ground. To those which are kept by force, to dream of a midwife signifies liberty. If a woman that is not with child dreameth of seeing her, it fore-showeth she will have a fit of sickness, of long continuance.

**MONSTER.** To see a monster or monstrous fish in the sea, is not good; but out of the sea every fish and great monster is good, because then they can hurt no more, or save themselves. And therefore, besides that our dream signifies that our enemies cannot hurt us, it saith moreover that the wicked shall be punished.

MOUNTAINS. To dream of mountains, valleys, woods, and plains, indicates heaviness, fears, and troubles; stripes to servants and malefactors, and hurt to the rich. It is always better to cross over them, and not to stay there, than to slumber by the way. To dream you ascend a very high mountain, signifies honor. If any dream that a mountain is fallen upon a valley, it signifies that some great lord will oppress and destroy good men. If you dream that when you arrive at the top of the mountain you catch a fall, and yet get no hurt thereby, it shows that though in your business you shall meet with some cross, yet you shall overcome it without damage.

MUCK. To dream of muck or dung is generally said to denote good. But this is certain, that to dream of muck is a certain sign that thou shalt be invited to a feast.

MULBERRY TREE. If one dreams he sees a mulberry tree, it signifies an increase, with abundance of goods and children.

MULE. To dream of the mule signifies malice and foolish imaginations. Artemidorus is of opinion that to dream of mules is good for all works, especially husbandry, only they cross weddings and increase; but to dream that mules are savage and mad, and that they do any hurt, argues deceit by some of our own house or subjects. "To dream that a mule carries books upon his back, and that those to whom they belong are divided, is a sign that the person so dreaming shall be disturbed in his devotions the next morning, " says a nameless author.

MUSIC. To dream you hear melodious music, which is even ready to ravish your ear, signifies that the party dreaming shall suddenly hear some very acceptable news, with which he shall be greatly delighted. But if people dream that they hear harsh, discordant notes, and ill-tuned music, it signifies the contrary; and they shall soon meet with such tidings as they do not care to hear. To dream that one hears charming music on a sudden, and yet cannot tell whence it comes, shows the party dreaming shall suddenly be surprised with some unexpected happiness.

# N

**NAG.** To dream that you ride on a white, gray, or dappled nag, signifies prosperity.

**NAILS.** To dream your nails are grown long is very good, and denotes riches, prosperity, and happiness, great success in love, a good industrious husband or wife, and dutiful children; it also foretells that you will suddenly receive a sum of money that will be of great use to you.

**NAVEL.** If anyone dreams that he hath a pain in his navel, if the grief be great he shall receive bad news of his father and mother, who will be in danger of death. If he hath neither father nor mother, he will lose his estate that came to him by father and mother, in the same proportion as the pain is, or else will be forced to forsake his native country.

**NAVEW-GENTLE.** To dream of eating the French navew-gentle denotes vain hope.

**NECK.** To dream of the neck signifies power, honor, riches, and inheritances. And every carbuncle, malady, or imperfection about the neck, head, or beard, signifies sickness indifferently to all.

**NETTLES.** To dream of nettles, and that you sting yourself with them, shows that you will venture hard for what you desire to obtain. And if young folks dream thus, it shows they are in love, and are willing to take a nettle, though they be stung thereby.

**NIGHT BIRDS.** To dream of any sort of night birds, as the owlet, the great owl, bittern, and bat, is ominous; and Anselmus Julianus advises those who have such dreams to undertake no business on the day following.

**NIGHTINGALE.** To dream of this pretty warbler is the forerunner of joyful news, great success in business, of plentiful crops, and of a sweet-tempered lover. For a married woman to dream of a nightingale, shows that she will have children who will be great singers. It signifieth also good work, and principally weddings and music, and promiseth a housewifely wife.

**NIGHTMARE.** To dream of being ridden by the nightmare is a sign that a woman so dreaming shall be suddenly after married; and that a man shall be ridden and domineered over by a fool.

**NOSE.** To dream one has a fair and great nose is good to all; for it signifies subtlety of sense, providence in affairs, and acquaintance with great personages. But to dream one has no nose, signifies the contrary; and to a sick man death, for dead men's heads have no nose. If anyone dreams his nose is longer than ordinary, he will become rich and powerful, provident and subtile, and be well received among grandees. To dream one has two noses signifies discord and quarrels, especially with his domestic kindred. If one dreams that his nose is grown so big that it is hideous to the sight, he will live in prosperity and abundance, but never gain the love of the people. If anyone dreams his nose is stopped, so that he hath lost his scent—if he be a king, he is in some imminent danger from him that hath the greatest authority about his person. If it be a private person, he is in danger of being deceived by his wife, who will commit herself with one of the servants.

**NOSEGAY.** To dream of gathering and making nosegays is unlucky, showing that our best hopes shall wither as flowers do in a nosegay. To dream of garlands is very good in the spring, but bad in the other seasons.

NUT TREES. To dream that you see nut-trees, and that you crack and eat their fruit, signifies riches and content, gained with labor and pains. To dream that you find nuts that have been hid signifies you will find some treasure.

## O

OAK. To dream that one sees a stately oak signifies to the dreamer riches, profit, and long life.

OFFICE. To dream that one is deposed and put out of his office, estate, place or dignity, is ill to the dreamer; and if he be sick, it shows he shall quickly die.

OIL. To dream of being anointed with oil, is good for all women, except those that are wicked; but for men it is ill, and signifies shame, except those who are accustomed to use it, as surgeons, painters, oilmen, and the like.

OLD WOMAN. To dream that you are courted by an old woman, and marry her, shows that you shall have good luck in prosecuting your affairs, and yet not without some reproaches from the world.

OLIVE TREE. To dream you see an olive tree with olives, denotes peace, delight, concord, liberty, dignity, and fruition of your desires. In dreams the olive tree signifies the wife principally, and liberty; and therefore it is good to dream that it is flourishing well, and bearing fair and ripe fruit in season. To dream you beat olives down is good for all but servants.

ONIONS. To dream of these useful vegetables denotes a mixture of good and ill luck. If you are eating them, you will receive some money, recover some lost or stolen thing, or discover some hidden treasure; your sweetheart will be faithful, but of a cross temper. It also denotes attacks from thieves and a failure of crops. If you are gathering onions, it betokens the receipt of some unexpected news of a joyful kind, the recovery of some sick person of your family, or a speedy removal from your present situation.

ORCHARDS. To dream of orchards, gardens, and flowery places is an emblem of pleasure; and if you dream that they abound with good fruit, it signifies abundance of riches and plenty; and if you dream also of many fountains in them, they signify pleasure and delight, with great store of wit. If you dream the trees be barren, it signifies the contrary.

ORGANS. To dream that you hear the sound of organs signifies joy.

OXEN. The ox in dreams signifies a profitable servant to his master, and shows the subject shall be brought under the yoke of obedience. If a man dreams that he sees fat oxen, it denotes a year of plenty; but if they be poor and lean, it threatens a year of scarcity and famine. To dream you see oxen plowing in the field is gain.

OYSTERS. To dream of opening oysters shows great hunger, which the party dreaming shall suddenly sustain; or else that he shall take pains for his living, as they do that open oysters.

## P

PALM. If one dreams that he sees or smells the palm, it signifies amity, prosperity, abundance, and good success in his enterprises. If it be a woman that dreams so, she shall bear children; if it be a maid, she will suddenly be married.

PAPER. To dream you write on paper, signifies an accusation made against you. To dream you read a paper, signifies news. To dream you blot or tear your paper, signifies the well-ordering of your business.

**PARTRIDGES.** To dream one sees partridges is a sign that a man shall have to do with women that are malicious, ungrateful, and void of conscience.

**PEACHES.** To dream of peaches, bastard peaches, and such kinds of fruit, in season, denotes to him that dreams he sees or eats them, content, health, and pleasure.

**PEAS.** To dream of peas well boiled denotes good success and expedition of business.

**PERFUMES.** If anyone dreams he perfumes his head with oils, essence, or sweet-scented powders, that signifies that he who dreams hath too great an opinion of himself, and will be haughty and vain-glorious in his demeanor to his associates. If it be a woman, she will deceive her husband and wear the breeches.

**PICTURES.** To dream one draws pictures is pleasure without profit.

**PIES.** To dream one makes pies is joy and profit.

**PIGEONS.** To dream you see pigeons is a good sign; to wit, that you will have content and delights at home, and success in affairs abroad. To dream you see a white pigeon flying, which is taken in the sacred writings for the hieroglyphic of the Holy Ghost, signifies consolation, devotion, and good success in undertakings, provided they are such as are for the glory of God and the good of our neighbors. Wild pigeons signify dissolute women, and tame pigeons denote honest women and matrons.

**PINE TREE.** To dream you see a pine tree denotes idleness and remissness.

**PLOUGH.** To dream of a plough is good for marriage, courtship, and such like affairs; but it requireth some time to bring them to perfection.

POLECAT. To dream a man has a polecat, shows he will love some ill-favored woman, by whom he will be bewitched.

POVERTY. To dream of being in necessity signifies some good to one; and yet this dream brings no good, but signifies crossfortune to those which make commodity of their tongue and fair speech.

PRECIPICES. To dream that one sees great and steep precipices, and that one falls over them, signifies that he that dreams will suffer much injury and hazard of his person, and his goods be in danger by fire.

PRESCRIBE. To dream that one prescribes medicine to the sick signifies profit and felicity.

## Q

QUAGMIRE. To dream one is fallen into a quagmire shows the party dreaming shall meet with such obstructions in his affairs as shall be very difficult to overcome.

QUAILS. To dream of quails signifies bad news from sea, debates, quarrels, piracy, ambuscades, and treachery.

QUEEN. To dream that you see the king or queen signifies honor, joy, and much prosperity.

QUICK. For a woman to dream that she is quick with child shows that she will be in danger of miscarriage, or that she will bring forth a dead child.

QUINCE. To dream of quinces signifies the dreamer shall meet with some changes in his affairs that shall be for the better.

## R

RACE. To dream of running a race is good to all, except they be sick persons when they dream they come to the end of their race, for it signifies that shortly they shall come to the end of their life.

RAINBOW. To dream you see a rainbow denotes the changing of your present estate and manner of life. To dream of seeing a rainbow in the East is a good omen to the poor and sick; for the former will recover their estates, and the latter their health. To dream of seeing a rainbow in the West, to the rich is a good, to the poor a bad sign. To dream you see the rainbow directly over your head, signifies a change of fortune, and most commonly the death of the dreamer and the ruin of his family. Note, also, that in your dreams the rainbow on the right hand is good, and on the left, ill; and you must judge the right or the left according to the sun. And in what quality soever it appears, it is a good sign to anyone that is afflicted with poverty or any other affliction, for it changeth the time and the air.

READING. To dream you are reading romances and comedies, or other diverting books, signifies joy and comfort. To dream you read serious books or books of divine science, signifies benediction and wisdom.

RICE. To dream of eating rice denotes abundance of instruction.

RIDGES. To dream of going on the ridges of houses is a sign that the party so dreaming is of a nice disposition; and if he happens to tread once awry, he shall fall to decay and so into great poverty.

## S

SABLE. To dream one is in a room hung with sable or mourning, shows the person dreaming shall quickly hear of the death of some near relation, or very good friend.

SACK-POSSET. To dream of eating a sack-posset signifies to women much gossiping; and to a man that he shall obtain his sweetheart, of whom a sack-posset is the emblem.

SACRILEGE. To dream that you commit sacrilege is a dream that is most ill to all, except it be to sacrificers and prophets, for by custom they receive and divide the first-fruits of oblations, and are always nourished by the gods.

SADDLE. To dream you are riding a horse without a saddle signifies poverty, disgrace, and shame to the dreamer.

SCHOOL. To dream you begin to go to school again, and you cannot say your lessons right, shows that you are about to undertake something which you do not well understand.

SEEING THE FACE OF GOD. To dream that you see the face of God, such as He reveals Himself to man, and that He seems to stretch forth His arms while we humbly invoke Him, signifies joy, comfort, grace, the blessing of God, and good success in business.

SHAKING. To dream you hear a shaking signifies deceit, which will happen to the dreamer in the place where he dreams.

SHE-GOAT. To dream you see or have many she-goats, sheep, cows, and horses, signifies wealth and plenty.

SILK. To dream you are clothed in silk, signifies honor. To dream that you trade with a stranger in silk, denotes profit and joy.

SILVER. If one dreams he gathers up silver, it signifies damage and loss. To see silver eaten signifies great advantage. To eat silver signifies wrath and anger.

SISTERS. To dream you see your deceased brethren and sisters signifies long life, but to dream you marry your sister's husband signifies danger.

TABLES. Playing at tables in dreams is the representation of a field prepared for the battle. The two gamesters are the generals, the tables are the field, and the men are the soldiers that make up the two armies; therefore, if anyone dreams that he plays tables with an acquaintance, it is a sign that he will fall out with somebody he loves; and if he dreams he wins, so he shall be victorious over his enemies; and, on the contrary, if he dreams he loseth, he will be worsted and overcome in the encounter. If the dreamer imagine he hath taken many of his men in play, it foretells that he will take many of his enemies prisoners.

TAPESTRY. To dream that one makes tapestry signifies joy, without very great reason for it.

TETTERS. If one dream he is full of tetters, it signifies he will grow rich in proportion to the tetters that signify his riches.

THIGHS. The thighs in dreams represent relations. If anyone dreams both his thighs are broken, or beaten black and blue, he will die in a foreign country alone, without the assistance of his relations.

TRANSMUTATION. In dreaming, to be changed from little to great, and again from great to be greater, so that you exceed not reason, is good, for it is increase of business and goods; but to be greater than common use is death. Also, it is ill for an old man to be changed into a young man, or a young man into a child, for they shall change to a worse estate; but the contrary is good, for they shall come to a better estate. To dream of being turned into a woman is very good for men in mean circumstances. Rich men who dream thus will meet with misfortunes; and such a dream is bad to all handicraftsmen whose labor is hard. If a woman dream that she is an unmarried man, without children, she will have both husband and children; but if married, and having children, she will die a widow. To be turned into brass shows some sudden quarrel and victory; it is good for military men. Iron shows hardness and misery. Clay or earth foretells dissolution; but those who deal in earthenware may reap good from such a dream. Rocks, stone, flint, etc., show continual hard usage, with mocks, reproaches, blows, and slanders. To dream that you are turned into a beast, shows that your nature partakes, or will partake, of the nature of that beast.

# V

VAULTS. To dream of being in hollow vaults, deep cellars, or the bottom of coal-pits, signifies matching with a widow; for he that marries her shall be a continual drudge, and yet shall never sound the depths of her policies.

VELVET. To dream you trade with a stranger in velvet, and other fine silks, signifies profit and joy.

VICTUALS. To dream of victuals, and that you eat a variety, signifies loss; for in dreams victuals and provisions signify the master of the house.

VINEGAR. To dream that you drink vinegar signifies sickness.

VIRGINALS. To dream one plays, or sees another play upon the virginals, signifies the death of relations or funeral obsequies.

# W

WALNUTS. To dream that one sees and eats walnuts or hazelnuts signifies difficulty and trouble.

WASPS. To dream you are stung by wasps, signifies vexation and trouble from envious persons.

**WETHERS.** To dream you see or have many wethers, sheep, she-goats, etc., signifies health and plenty.

**WRESTLING.** We read of Jacob's wrestling with an angel in a dream; he, therefore, that dreams he is very forward to wrestle with another person shows some contention will follow, and that he will be outdone by some of his acquaintances in worldly affairs. A woman who dreams she wrestles with her husband, will certainly bring shame and sorrow into the family. For children to wrestle with men is good. Wrestling in a dream with death denotes a long sickness and lawsuits.

**WRITE.** To dream one writes on paper signifies accusation.

# A NOD IN PASSING TO MR. FREUD

## CHAPTER III

With all due deference to the genius of such psychologists as Freud, Jung and Adler, it must be admitted that a great deal of bunk has been written on the sexual significance of dreams. People are coming more and more to a realization of this fact. Defenders of the Freudian theories attribute this disbelief—much of which comes from the medical profession—to the conservatism that is shown by the majority of doctors. Perhaps, however, it is just a matter of common sense.

Freud's professional standing was such that he secured the attention of students of psychology, including doctors of medicine, sociologists and other people of more or less intelligence, but his radical theories regarding sex in dreams got their largest acceptance from those who either were themselves over-sexed (and liked to talk about it), or who were the kind of people who naturally followed the latest fad, whether it was contract bridge, crossword puzzles or badminton.

Far be it from me to dismiss lightly all of Freud's theories. I do not dismiss any of them on puritanical grounds. A grown person who shies away from the subject of sex or its decent discussion and implications should be recommended for treatment by a competent psychiatrist.

From a normal viewpoint, it seems a very natural thing to dream of sex and its various manifestations, both psychological and physiological. In a world peopled almost entirely by males and females, it could hardly be otherwise. Sex, we may assume, is here to stay.

On the other hand, there are fundamentals like food, shelter, clothing, warmth, curiosity, fear, etc., each with related branches, none of which is primarily connected with sex. Yet among the psychologists are those who, through a system of symbols reduce the matter of dreaming to outcroppings of sex urges, repressions, expressions and depressions. Based on the sex significance of a carving knife, Franklin P. Adams, the well-known columnist, lampooned the idea in some whimsical verses beginning:

> "Don't tell me what you dreamed last night,
> For I've been reading Freud."

No one could take exception to the manner in which it was expressed but to one acquainted with Freud's theories it was nothing less than Rabelaisian.

All of this seems rather amusing, and not very important, to a person who has studied the interpretation of dreams from the learning and experience of age-old authorities. If, in the Freudian psychology, a knife has a phallic implication, it can quite as logically—and I believe much more so —be regarded as significant of a cutting apart; in other words, a separation. It implies pain or sorrow, or possible improvement through the removal of a diseased part.

The entrance to a cave suggests sex in the modern psychological scheme, but to the well balanced thinking mind the implication would more likely be mystery, adventure, danger, terror, or perhaps oblivion. Certain of these subjects might, indeed, be connected in some way with sex, but so might anything in a world which moves and develops through human relationships between men and women.

Mr. Freud has stated* that dreams which are conspicuously innocent invariably embody coarse erotic wishes, and I sincerely trust that anyone who believes that will send me a ten dollar bill. In the same book he also says that there is no series of associations which cannot be adapted to the representation of sexual facts. Dreams which are "conspicuously innocent" in Mr. Freud's notion appear to be those which have no connection with sex, and right thinking people resent the implication that sex is unclean.

*Dream Psychology. By Sigmund Freud. New York: The James A. McCann Company. 1921.

Some of the erotic symbols that Freud suggests are given herewith. It is my opinion that they make a good case for the dream interpretations based on experience and common sense.

Female symbols are doors, boxes, caves, small cases, caskets, closets, stoves. A lock is female, while a key is male. Male symbols include sticks, tree trunks, umbrellas, sharp weapons, knives, daggers, pikes, nail files. The male genital is symbolized by a woman's hat, a man's cravat, complicated machines and apparatus, landscapes in which there are bridges or wooded mountains, children, flying machines, relatives.

A row of rooms signifies a brothel; the right hand is a symbol of righteousness, marriage, or relations with a prostitute; while the left hand indicates homosexuality or worse. It is no wonder that Franklin P. Adams wrote "Don't tell me what you dreamed last night." Nor is it any wonder that people are looking for dream interpretations to those who base them on the ancient and honorable authorities whose line was established a thousand or more years before the pyramids of Egypt were even thought of.

# LOVE DREAMS

## CHAPTER IV

It is probable that of all dreams those pertaining to love, either between man and maidens or within the married state, are the most interesting, for, as the poet has said, it is love that makes the world go round. It is more important, more vital, more thrilling than money, honor, or even food. It is stimulating alike to youth, middle age, and old age. Its implications are not necessarily physical. It may be brotherly love; it may be affection for a friend, a companion, or a parent. It may be love on only a spiritual plane. One who has never loved is indeed a useless member of society, and there are few who come in this category.

This division of the book deals largely with romantic love, and it is probable that it will be referred to more than any other, for at the time of life when most individuals have not yet found a mate the subject is one of paramount interest.

The following interpretations are based on ancient findings and they are, moreover, based on average people's experience. Those who are by nature suspicious, even in their love affairs, should not allow this phase of their individuality to color their dream interpretations, for it should be remembered that, above all, love is trust.

## LOVE PORTENTS

### A

ABANDONMENT. *Of your lover* indicates that you will not find something valuable that you have lost; and that advances made to those you believed your friends will be repulsed.

*Of your mistress* is a portent of the inheritance of a fortune that you have not previously expected.

ACCORDION. *Hearing* dance music from this instrument means that you will be happy with the man or woman you love.

*Playing* sweet music indicates that your loving embraces will be returned with sincerity; but if the instrument seems to be out of tune, there will be either a quarrel or unfaithfulness.

ACCOUNTS (*See* Adding Machine Ledger). Bookkeeping dreams may augur difficulty in love affairs, but they usually point to eventual success. Difficulty in adding figures or in balancing accounts is an indication of quarrels, but to dream that a balance is secured at the first trial is a prediction of an early marriage.

ACROBAT (*See* Danger). Here is a warning of a rival for the object of your affections, but, unless the acrobat falls, the rival will not be successful. To dream of being an acrobat is a presage of success in an important undertaking.

ACTOR OR ACTRESS (*See* Stage, Play, Singer). There is no particular significance in dreaming of actors or actresses except as they may represent art in depicting emotion of one kind or another.

*Love scenes* indicate that your sweetheart will be jealous of you.

*Tragedy* portends quarrels.

*Comedy* foretells a change in your financial condition, either for better or worse.

*Cynicism* points toward difficulties with one of the opposite sex.

*Burlesque* is an augury of illness.

AIRPLANE. *Piloting* means that your destiny is under your control and that if you exercise your best judgment, you will be successful in any enterprise on which you may embark. If difficulties arise in such a dream, be prepared to encounter them in your enterprise, but do not be daunted, for you will succeed through your determination. Indicates a successful marriage for a man.

*Riding* in an airplane with the object of your affections foretells a happy married life.

*Seeing* one or more airplanes is an augury of an improvement in either your financial condition or your love affairs, perhaps both.

ALABASTER. Success and a happy marriage, unless the article of alabaster is broken, which is a harbinger of ill luck.

ALBUM. A new admirer is indicated to the young woman who dreams of looking at a photograph album.

ALUM. This tart, puckery substance, tasted in a dream, indicates that the person will meet a dilemma of a very puzzling nature, especially as regards love affairs. If the alum turns sweet in the mouth, there will be a satisfactory solution of the problem involved.

AMETHYST. *Seeing* an amethyst ring, brooch or necklace foretells a calm married life.

*Losing* one of these is indicative of trouble in love affairs.

*Receiving* a gift of an amethyst is a forerunner of good luck in every direction.

ANTELOPE. To see an antelope stumble or fall is a sign that you have aspired to greater heights in love or business than you can achieve.

ARCHITECT. If she dreams of seeing an architect at work, a girl of marriageable age may expect to encounter difficulties in finding a suitable mate.

A married person of either sex who dreams of seeing an architect drawing plans should consider it a warning of both financial and marital difficulties.

73

**ARROW.** To dream of seeing an arrow shot straight to its mark is an omen of achievement in your fondest anticipation. A broken arrow, or one shot wide of the mark, predicts failure.

**ASP** *(See* Snake, Reptile). Sweethearts would do well to regard this as a warning against suspicion. If, however, the dreamer kills the asp, it signifies that any impending difficulty will be overcome. It is bad fortune to dream of being bitten by an asp.

**AUGUST.** No good comes of dreaming that you are to be wed, or are actually wed, in August. The chances are that your early married life will be beset by many difficulties of adjustment.

**AUTUMN.** Happiness through understanding is foretold by a dream of being married in autumn.

To meet a lover in the autumn forest, with the leaves of the trees brightly colored, is a sure sign of success in love.

**AXE.** A keen, serviceable axe indicates that your lover, husband or wife will be worthy.

A much battered, nicked, rusty or broken axe foretells irresponsibility on the part of loved ones; also unfortunate investments.

# B

**BABY.** A successful climax to your love affair is indicated by your dreaming of a lovely baby. It also indicates that you will have many good friends.

A baby who cries, is fretful or vomits, or otherwise appears to be suffering, or is ill nourished, augurs disappointment in matters of the heart.

For a lover to call you "baby" in your dreams is indicative of a change in your love affairs or unfaithfulness on the part of one you have trusted. It indicates a light-hearted attitude toward the love in which you have believed.

BACKHOUSE. This is a good omen for women in love. It foretells new lovers to a maiden, and increase in her family to a wife, and an impending marriage to a widow.

BALCONY. A lover who dreams of a sad leavetaking on a balcony may look forward to a period of stress, which may include sickness, the activities of a rival, or jealousy in one form or another.

BALLET. A dream of seeing a ballet performed on a stage portends infidelity on the part of someone you love. This will lead to jealousy and quarrels. To dream of talking with a ballet dancer in a dressing room is also a sign of an impending quarrel with husband, wife or lover.

BANANAS. Those who are in love should be warned by dreaming of eating this fruit, for it is an omen that they are in danger of picking the wrong mate. To see bananas growing in a dream, especially if the great leaves are waving in the wind, is an excellent sign for lovers. To dream of picking them from the tree and eating them should be regarded as a caution to go slowly in any enterprise whatever.

BANJO. If a young woman sees a Negro playing a banjo, she will be likely to have quarrels with her lover.

BEAR. Rivals in love are indicated by a dream of bears. If, however, a bear is seen climbing a tree, a happy outcome of the problem is to be expected.

BEARD (*See* Shaving). To dream of having a full luxuriant beard on the face is to be able to look forward to great success, both in money matters and in love.
    To clip one's beard foretells loss of a financial nature or the loss of a sweetheart. To clip another's beard portends a quarrel.

75

A young woman who dreams of admiring a beard is threatened with an unwise marriage; but if she dreams of having a beard herself, the prediction is that she will soon be a bride, if unmarried, or a mother if she has a husband.

BEAUTY. This is a good omen in the main, but it must be interpreted in connection with the accompanying incidents. A beautiful woman ordinarily betokens happiness in love or in marriage; but mere beauty of face and form combined with ugliness of character (*see* Harlot, Prostitute, Demimondaine) foretells degradation and loss through the worship of false gods.

BED. If a woman dreams of making a bed, there is a thrilling, though not necessarily respectable, love affair in the offing. For a man to have this dream indicates that something he would wish hidden will be found out.

BEDROOM. An ultra-luxurious, highly scented bedchamber foretells very unusual changes in the mode of life, and indicates that both young men and young women should guard their actions with the utmost circumspection.

To dream of being in such a room with one of the opposite sex is direct warning against promiscuous friendships, especially if an amorous situation between unmarried people should develop.

BIRDS. To dream of a mourning dove or a hoot owl is an omen of deep unhappiness through the ill fortune of one you love.

Colorful plumage on any bird of which you dream means that your life partner will have wealth and you will be happy. It is indicative of a successful ending to a love affair.

BONNET. (*See* Head). If a man dreams of a woman trying her bonnet, or putting on a hat, there is good luck to be expected in his wooing.

If a woman dreams of a man trying on a woman's hat, she is likely to suffer great embarrassment.

BOSOM. If a girl dreams that her lover, or any other man, is glancing covertly at her partly revealed bosom, she will have to be on her guard against over-amorous advances which will be made to her.

For an unmarried man to dream of a woman's bosom is a sign that he will contract a happy marriage; for a married man, that his wife will inherit property from an unexpected source.

BOTTLES. Dreams in which bottles figure prominently signify many different things, depending on the size, color and shape, and on the contents.

Bottles of transparent glass filled with clear, colorless liquid are of good omen, especially to lovers. If the liquid is murky, there are quarrels ahead. If there is sediment, it is a prophecy of disappointment.

Bottles of unusual color foretell exciting adventures, which may be dangerous if the bottles are full, or merely irritating if they are empty.

Wine bottles covered with dust or cobwebs are a prediction of a long and happy life. To see them broken is a warning of the loss of a friend or lover.

Oddly shaped bottles are a presage of a proposal from a wholly unexpected source.

BRACELET. A happy marriage that will occur soon is foretold if you dream of wearing a bracelet given you by a friend.

BRASSIERE. For a woman to dream of putting on a brassiere is an indication that she will have an irksome experience with her husband or lover. If one or both of the straps break, it is an omen of disillusionment.

BRICKS. Bricks, either singly, piled or in a wall, point toward a disagreement with your lover. If you are laying them and you have no trouble in making them even, the disagreement will not be serious.

BRIDE. Happiness is indicated by any dream of a bride, but if the bride happens to be weeping, it portends vexing circumstances in connection with the dreamer's in-laws.

To be a bride foretells an inheritance in the form of an annuity.

Kissing a bride means that you will be reconciled with someone you have quarreled with.

Kissing one's own bride foretells a happy solution of a pressing problem.

Catching a bridal bouquet in a dream, as well as in fact, is a sign that the unmarried will find a mate within the year.

Seeing a bridal procession with bridesmaids indicates a sure turn for the better in both your love and financial affairs.

Seeing a bride wearing white and a veil is a promise of a happy married life. If she wears traveling clothes, it is probable that you will have to make an important decision shortly.

BRIDEGROOM. Responsibility and care are indicated by this dream. A laughing bridegroom portends faithlessness on your part or on the part of some valued friend.

BRIDESMAID. Unhappiness is foretold by a dream of being a bridesmaid, but good luck in seeing bridesmaids.

To dream of being a bridesmaid and stepping on the bride's train is a forerunner of a very embarrassing experience.

BRONZE. Failure in love is betokened by dreaming of bronze statuary. To see a bronze statue come to life foretells a serious love affair that will not culminate in marriage.

BROTH (SEE also Soup). Eating broth augurs well for those in love, for their future will be one of great felicity.

BUTTERFLY (See Insects). A white butterfly on the wing predicts much innocent pleasure with one of the opposite sex. If the butterfly alights, even for a moment, it means that lasting love will be yours.

Butterflies of gorgeous colors indicate that someone you thought indifferent loves you deeply.

A black butterfly betokens inconstancy on the part of your sweetheart.

BUTTONS. *Finding* a button is an omen of good luck in business or in love.

*Losing* one foretells extreme embarrassment or other vexatious, though not necessarily serious happening, in connection with an affair you may have.

*Sewing* on buttons—particularly if the garment is an item of underwear—points to happiness, honor and wealth.

*Using*, or buttoning up, is an indication of the successful termination of your highest ambition. Unbuttoning foretells that you will shortly begin an important enterprise that may hamper or postpone a projected marriage.

## C

CALLING. To hear a recognized voice in a dream, if it is from a dead person, is to be regarded as a portent of a difficulty with a friend, lover, or relative, which may be avoided or cleared up by using your best judgment. The significance of the dream, of course, depends on the words one hears—whether warning or reassuring in their tone.

The voice of a living person heard in a dream foretells exciting news, which may be either pleasant or distressing according to what is said and the manner of speaking.

CAMP. A camp in the woods signifies a release from some pressing care, and the solution of a lover's difficulties.

A military camp means that an unmarried woman will be likely to marry the first man who proposes to her; while to a man it signifies success in his business or investments.

CANAL. If a woman dreams of floating smoothly along a canal in a rowboat or canoe, it is an indication that her married life will be happy and that she and her husband will be true to each other.

CANARY BIRDS. To hear canaries singing is a sign of the utmost happiness in your love. This applies equally to both single and married folk, even though at the time the outlook may appear unfavorable.

CANDLES. To see a lighted candle is a harbinger of comfortable circumstances both in love and other fortunes. An especially bright light denotes a sudden change for the better. An extinguished candle portends the death of someone you hold dear. A short, guttering candle about to die out means that your lover will deceive you.

An unmarried woman who dreams of molding candles will have a surprising offer of marriage. If she lights a candle, she will have a secret meeting with her lover.

CANNON. A maiden who hears the noise of cannonading, or sees cannon, will marry a soldier and will be left behind when he is on duty. A man who has this dream will be unsettled.

CANNON BALLS. This bodes no good to either sex. You will be beset by trials that at the time will be incomprehensible. The same applies to the shells of high-powered guns. Singly, they mean vexations; in stacks or cases, they portend real troubles.

CANDY. For a young woman to receive candy is a sign that she will have ardent attentions from a much older man. To a man it signifies prosperity. If either a man or a woman sends bonbons to a person of either sex, it is an indication that a favorite plan will miscarry.

CANOE. To be in a canoe on smooth waters with your beloved is a presage of happiness in love and early marriage. In the case of married folk, it signifies freedom from worry. If the waters are rough, quarrels will come, but they are not necessarily fated to have a serious ending.

CAP. A maiden who sees her lover wearing a cap will find it difficult to be herself when next she sees the man of her choice. She will be either suspicious or bashful, or both.

For either sex to be presented with a cap of any kind is a presage of romance, either legal or illicit.

To put a cap on the head is a warning to be extremely careful in any love affairs.

CAPE. Seeing a woman or girl wearing a cape foretells that you will have an experience that you may wish to keep a secret. A man wearing a cape is a harbinger of prosperity.

CAPER. To dream of children or young animals—kittens, puppies, calves, etc.—capering is a forerunner of a happy marriage and freedom from worry.

CAPTIVE. For a girl to dream that she is held a captive is an indication that her lover or husband will resent any attentions or courtesies that other men may show her. A man having this dream may expect failure in a business deal.

CAPTAIN. A man who dreams of being a captain in the army will do well to accept responsibility, for through it his wealth will increase. An unmarried woman who dreams of meeting a captain may look forward to marrying a handsome and prosperous man.

CARDS (*See* Gambling Games, Poker). To dream that your sweetheart is a card player is an indication that you should be very sure that his or her attitude toward you is above reproach.

If you yourself are playing cards in a dream, it is a sign that you will be in danger of making a mistake in some love affair, unless the cards that you hold are mostly hearts, which combination points decisively to a happy married life.

**CARNIVAL.** If you dream of being at a carnival and grotesque figures in masks come within your vision, there will be either matrimonial discord or unsatisfactory developments in a love affair.

**CARPET.** A luxurious home with servants is in store for the young man or woman who dreams of carpets.

**CARROTS.** Eating carrots signifies success in any undertaking, including marriage and parenthood, because you will have the fortitude to make it successful.

**CART.** If lovers dream of riding together in a horse-drawn cart or motor truck, they will be sure to overcome any difficulties that may befall them.

**CASTLE.** *Living in* is an indication that you will have a suitor who is undesirable.

*Entering* is a premonition of marriage with someone you have known only a short time.

*Leaving* a castle alone betokens the breaking of an engagement; with a party, it is the sign of a quarrel that may or may not turn out disastrously.

*Seeing* a castle forecasts an impending change in your circumstances, either in love affairs or in finances.

**CATERPILLAR.** No good may be expected by lovers from dreaming of seeing caterpillars. To kill one is a sign that your affair will be broken off. To find one on your person predicts a disagreeable experience with someone you regarded as a friend.

**CATTLE** (*See also* Ox). To dream of milking a cow is an indication that you will be fortunate in both business and love, in proportion to the amount of milk secured. If the cow proves to be dry, or nearly so, coolness is likely to develop in your affair of the heart, and your business will probably decline.

It is a fortunate augury to see calves in a dream, and yearlings indicate prosperity.

**CATS.** Deceit and treachery on the part of people you have trusted are foretold by a dream of cats, but to dream of driving them away is a prediction that you will overcome your enemies.

**CAULIFLOWER** (*See* Cabbage and Vegetables). This vegetable appears to have no amatory significance except to young women, who, if they see it growing, will marry through pressure brought from outside sources, probably their parents.

**CAVE OR CAVERN.** A young woman who enters a cave in a dream is in danger of marrying a man of doubtful reputation, who will become her suitor in a mysterious manner.

A married woman or a man having this dream should be on guard against scandalous gossip.

**CELERY.** To dream of eating crisp celery, white or green, presages good health and happiness in love and marriage. Limp celery is an omen of misfortune.

**CELLAR.** The condition and contents, as well as the odor, govern the significance of this dream.

A wine cellar portends marriage with a person of gambling instincts or one in a hazardous occupation.

A cellar well stored with foods, canned foods, fruits or vegetables, is an indication of success in business or love, or both.

A musty cellar indicates disappointment.

Being unable to get out of a cellar foretells that you will find yourself with difficulties of a serious nature.

**CHAMBER** (*See* Bedroom).

**CHAMBERMAID.** If a man dreams of making advances to a chambermaid, he should guard himself against indiscreet conduct, for he is otherwise likely to find himself in an embarrassing situation.

**CHAPEL.** A young person of either sex who dreams of going into a chapel is likely to have misfortune in love affairs. It implies disappointment at the least.

**CHEATING.** For a married person to dream that he or she has been cheating in love is a sign of trouble ahead. To dream that one has overcome a temptation to cheat predicts happiness.

Misfortune in love affairs is predicted by unmarried folk when they dream that they are cheated in card or other games or in business transactions.

**CHESTNUTS.** Eating chestnuts, raw, boiled or roasted, is a dream of good fortune in love affairs. An unmarried woman who has this dream will make a good marriage with a man who will be faithful and reasonably successful in business. Men who have this dream will have devoted wives.

**CHICKENS.** Those who see chickens in their dreams will have to fight the influence of someone they have suspected.

Eating chicken is a prediction that someone's selfishness will bring unpleasantness into your love affair.

**CHOIR.** If a man dreams of singing in a choir, he may expect success through addressing audiences.

A woman who has this dream should avoid jealousy, especially of any attention that her lover or husband may happen to pay to another.

**CHURCHYARD.** Good health is likely to follow this dream, but there will also be disappointment in matters pertaining to the heart.

**CIRCLE.** Whoever dreams of a circle should carefully avoid committing any indiscretion that might possibly influence their marital happiness.

**CLAMS.** Lucky is the maiden who dreams of eating clams

in company with her sweetheart. She will be likely to marry soon and have many children.

COCK CROWING. To dream of hearing a cock crowing is a prediction of an early marriage and a plentiful supply of money.

COINS. If a silver coin is given to a single person, the indication is that an engagement will be broken; while a gold coin signifies distress through the introduction of a rival.

COMBAT. An unmarried woman dreaming of seeing two men fighting may look forward to having two suitors, between whom she will find it difficult to choose.

COMPLETION. If a maiden dreams of finishing a dress, hat or other article of wearing apparel, it indicates that she will shortly give an answer to a proposal. A married woman having this dream may expect a small inheritance.

CONCERT. A symphony orchestra with many instruments predicts a harmonious married life. If there are soloists, either instrumental or vocal, it is a sign that your children will be successful.

A jazz or swing orchestra playing in a dream foretells nervous exhaustion through worry over love affairs.

A concert of old-fashioned melodious numbers is a promise of relief from worry, whether about love or finances.

CONVENTION. Gossip is likely to cause you and your lover grief if you dream of attending a convention. This dream also denotes that there will be some unusual development in your business affairs.

CONVICTS. Young women who dream of their lovers wearing convicts' uniforms may expect a disagreeable revelation.

To see a group of convicts marching, or a chaingang at work, is a portent of misfortune.

CORKS. Recorking a bottle of half-used liquid points toward a love affair that will not last long but will be intense.

Trying to insert too large a cork in a bottle indicates that the enterprise you may be considering will prove to be beyond your powers of accomplishment.

Breaking a cork while withdrawing it means disappointment in love.

Pushing a cork inside a bottle foreshadows a divorce in your immediate circle of friends.

Removing the cork from a champagne bottle is an indication that you will come under the influence of acquaintances who are light-hearted and untrustworthy.

CORN. Green corn growing foretells a happy married life, with healthy and joyous children.

To dream of eating it from the cob is a prediction of success in money matters.

Popping corn in a dream is propitious if the popping is brisk and the corn is white; but if it burns, the prediction is toward an opposite state of affairs.

CORNS. Bad news for lovers is foretold by a dream of a painful corn on a toe of the right foot. If the corn is on the left foot, it is a warning against scandal.

COURTSHIP. This is an unlucky dream for a girl, but lucky for a man. To dream of being courted by a handsome youth is usually a sign pointing to spinsterhood. To dream of courting a pretty girl predicts happiness for a bachelor; but a married man who has this dream should be on his guard against designing women.

CRABS. Catching crabs in a dream indicates a complicated state of affairs in a courtship or in matrimony, though not necessarily beyond hope of solution. Eating crabs is an indication that selfishness is likely to get you into difficulties. Seeing them displayed for sale predicts that a mystery will shortly cause you great concern.

CREAM. Foretells an early and successful marriage to lovers who have this dream; to others it is a presage of various good fortune and consequent happiness.

CROCKERY (*See* Dishes). To young lovers this is a favorable dream. By it is predicted an early marriage with a desirable partner. If the crockery is soiled, it is probable that some objection will have to be swept away before the marriage can take place.

CROSSROADS. To be at a crossroads in a dream predicts that lovers will soon have to make a momentous decision.

CRUCIFIX. It is good fortune for a girl to dream of wearing a crucifix, for she will be loved for her modesty and charm.

CURBSTONE. A lover who dreams of stepping up a curbstone may look forward to a happy mating with a faithful partner. Stepping down a curbstone is a foreboding of many difficulties in love and marriage.

CUSHIONS. *Lying on* cushions foretells an experience wherein luxury is secured at the expense of some high quality of character. It is a warning against light love affairs.

*Seeing* cushions portends a successful love affair for the unmarried; and happiness for those who are wedded.

Making a cushion predicts improvement in love affairs or business.

CUSTARD. For anyone to dream of *eating* custard out of a cup foretells a meeting with a stranger of great charm who may prove to be either a lifelong friend or a future mate.

Spilling custard, or throwing it, is usually the precursor of scandal regarding your love affairs.

# D

DANCING. Unmarried folk may regard this as a forerunner of a solution of their love problems. It is a fortunate dream also for married people, for they may look forward to much pleasure and pride in their children.

DANCING SCHOOL. Strange experiences with the opposite sex may be expected by those who dream of attending a school for dancing. Social or ballroom dancing instruction is connected with private affairs, while classic, tap, or other exhibition dancing with appearances in public.

DANCING TEACHER. If a girl dreams that her betrothed is a dancing teacher, she will have a good reason to suspect him.

DANDELION. A rich show of blossoming dandelions is a good omen for those who are in love, but blossoms that have gone to seed portend trouble ahead.

DANGER (*See* various causes of danger). Lovers who dream of being in danger will have to use the greatest care and discretion in all that they do to prevent their warning from coming true. It is frequently the precursor of a shattered romance.

DATES. *Eating* means that there will be a marriage between persons in your own group. You may be one of the contracting parties.
*Making* "dates" with friends is an augury of a disappointment in a business deal.

DECK. It is good luck for lovers to dream of being together on the deck of a ship or boat of any size.

DEER (*See also* Fawn). Lovers who dream of deer, particularly fawns, may look forward to a deep and lasting affair that will culminate in a happy marriage.

For a young man or a young woman to dream of killing a deer is an indication of the breaking up of a love affair.

DELIGHT (*See also* causes of delight). Dreams of delight over some action by a sweetheart are forerunners of a pleasure that is unexpected.

DEVOTION. A dream of devotion to religious or other duties is a prevision of a faithful and loving mate. It predicts understanding, tolerance, and a happy disposition on the part of both husband and wife.

DEW. Marriage with a person in very comfortable circumstances is to be expected by a single man or woman who dreams of seeing dew sparkling on grass. To walk barefooted in the dew betokens a pleasant surprise.

DIAMONDS. A good omen when a maiden dreams of being given diamonds in any form or setting, the indication being a marriage with a gentleman of high position and much wealth.

An unmarried man who dreams of giving diamonds to his sweetheart should exercise care in the selection of a mate. He should look for a young woman who is a homemaker rather than a society bud.

Either man or woman who dreams of wearing diamonds may expect a disagreeable experience with someone they believed a friend.

DICE. To dream of a lover throwing dice is to foresee unworthy actions on his or her part. If a lucky combination is thrown it is a sign of temporary success, but is not to be regarded as lucky as it may hurt someone dear to. you.

DINING. A quarrel may be expected if one dreams of dining with his or her lover in company with other persons. If the two right people are alone, it is a presage of an early marriage.

89

**DISASTER** (*See* Danger). To dream of being in a disaster of any kind foretells the loss of a lover, either through misunderstanding or an accident.

**DISHES** (*See* Crockery). Clean dishes, neatly arranged on shelves or tables, are lucky to dream about, especially for a maiden in love.

Soiled or broken dishes predict misfortune in affairs of the heart.

**DISINHERITED.** A young man may expect through this dream of being disinherited that his family will approve of the girl with whom he is in love.

**DIVING.** Lovers who dream of diving together into pleasant waters will be likely to find consummation of their passionate love within the year.

**DIVIDENDS.** Receiving dividends on an investment augurs well for those who look forward to marriage. Failing to receive expected dividends denotes the opposite.

**DIVORCE.** A warning dream. For those who are already married it means that they should try to use their understanding to the best advantage in order to avoid discord. For those in love, it warns against jealousy.

**DOGS.** If a dog bites you, it signifies a quarrel with your lover.

For an unmarried woman to fondle a small pet dog means that your sweetheart will turn out to be a "sissy."

To be frightened at a large dog is a sign that the unmarried person will have an affair with a person of large mental equipment.

A white dog, of whatever breed, will, if it appears friendly, be the precursor of a victory either in business or in love.

**DOLPHINS.** This is a bad dream for lovers. It denotes the loss of a sweetheart.

**DOME.** You will never get anywhere with the object of your affections if you dream of seeing a dome from a distance.

**DONKEY.** Lovers may expect difficulties through the machinations of evil women.

To be kicked by a donkey indicates that you will be found out if you carry on a clandestine love affair.

To be thrown off a donkey is a sign that you will have a lovers' quarrel.

To be presented with one is an indication of good luck in both business and marriage.

A white donkey in a dream foretells success in every undertaking—social, marital, and financial.

**DOOMSDAY.** To dream that the end of the world has come is a sign to lovers that the object of their affections will prove unsuitable as a mate.

**DOVE.** *Flying* denotes reconciliation of lovers who have quarreled.

*Feeding* is an augury of a happy outcome to a love affair.

A *dead* dove portends the death or unfaithfulness of a husband or wife.

**DUET.** *Singing or playing with one of the opposite sex* predicts marriage with the object of your affections.

*Singing or playing with one of the same sex* foretells an ending to your love affair.

*Hearing* a duet, either vocal or instrumental, is a fortunate dream for lovers to have.

**DUNGHILL.** A maiden who dreams of this may look forward to a marriage with a wealthy suitor.

**DUST.** Being covered with dust in a dream indicates that you will be jilted by your lover. To married folk it foretells serious vexations through their relatives or in-laws.

ELBOWS. For an eligible woman to dream of noticing particularly that a person has attractive elbows portends marriage in the near future with a man of substance both in matters of the mind and worldly goods.

If the elbows are distinctly unattractive, whether by malformation or dirt, she will be unfortunate either through being jilted or through marrying the wrong man.

ELOPEMENT. No good will come to either married or unmarried people from dreaming of a runaway marriage. It is a harbinger of disappointment and unfaithfulness and at the same time a warning that the dreamer's actions are such that he must mend his ways in order to avoid trouble.

To dream that your lover has eloped with someone else is an indication that he or she needs to be tested in order to be sure that an approaching marriage is a wise course.

EMBRACE. Usually quarrels may be expected from a dream wherein lovers embrace each other, although there may be governing factors in such a dream that would predict the reverse.

EMBROIDERY. A man who dreams of seeing someone embroidering or who dreams of seeing embroidered garments will have a wife whose wisdom and economy will be outstanding. It is good luck in matters of the heart for a woman to dream of embroidering.

EMERALD. For a lover to dream of seeing his fiancee wearing emeralds means that he will be jilted for a man of greater wealth.

ENGAGEMENT. You will not be married for a long time if you dream that you are engaged.

If you dream that you are breaking an engagement,

you will have to guard yourself against making a wrong decision in a matter of grave importance.

ERRANDS. A maid who sends someone on an errand in a dream may regard this as an omen that through her indifference she will lose her lover.

EVENING. It is bad luck for lovers to dream of walking together in the evening. It foretells a lovers' quarrel that can be patched up only after a long, painful misunderstanding.

EXCHANGE. If a young woman should dream of exchanging sweethearts with a friend, it is an indication that the probabilities are she would make a better marriage with another man.

EYE. There is a rival in the offing if a lover dreams of seeing a large human eye. It is a warning that he should watch his step if he is to make a happy marriage.

EYEGLASSES. If a maiden sees her lover wearing eyeglasses it is an omen of a termination of their affair.

# F

FACE. A person dreaming of an ugly face will have a quarrel with his or her best beloved.

A lover who dreams of seeing his sweetheart's face ten, twenty, or thirty years hence foretells a separation.

Unhappiness is foretold by a dream of seeing one's own face. If the dreamer is married there is a great possibility of divorce.

FAILURE. A lover who dreams that he fails to win the consent of a girl to be his wife will do well to pursue his suit with much more energy than heretofore, for if he does he will win her love and esteem.

FAIR. A young woman who dreams of being at a fair will

have a man of jovial disposition and sound principles for a husband.

FAITHLESS. Here is a dream which has an opposite significance to that which might be expected. A happy marriage is signified by a dream that a lover is faithless.

FALCON. If you are a young woman and dream of hunting with a falcon, it portends that a rival in love will try to undermine your reputation by calumny.

FAN. A fan has pleasant connotions. A maiden who dreams of fanning herself or being fanned by someone else will be likely to have a new lover.

To lose an old fan with either sentimental or historic associations indicates that her lover is becoming cold.

FAN DANCING. Suspicion is indicated by a dream in which a fan dancer performs. Either a man or a woman having this dream should beware of unseemly conduct that may lead to criticism from jealous people.

FAREWELL. A maiden who bids farewell to her lover will find very shortly that he will show growing indifference. If in this farewell she is indifferent to its significance and takes it as a matter of course, it is a sign that she will find another comforter ere long.

FAWN. (*See* Deer). A young married person dreaming of a fawn has every reason to expect that his or her lover will show the utmost in faithfulness.

FAWN ON. If you dream of being fawned on by someone who might expect to receive unusual favors it is a warning to avoid committing yourself when you are approached with an unusual proposition.

FENCE. Success in matters of the heart is denoted when a young woman dreams of building a fence.

Failure to hold the man she loves is foretold if she

dreams that the fence falls over or that she falls from the fence.

FIGHT. If a maiden sees her best beloved engaged in fighting with another man, it is an omen that he will prove unworthy.

If a man dreams of seeing his lady love fighting with another woman, it is a sign that she will prove a competent housewife.

FIGS. To dream of seeing figs growing on a tree is a sign that the dreamer will marry within a short time and that his or her state will be considerably improved through this marriage.

FINGERS. To dream of beautiful hands with white-tipped fingers and well-shaped but uncolored nails is a portent of requited love and many beautiful children.

FISH. It is lucky for a young woman to dream of seeing or catching fish for it is a sure sign that she will have an exceedingly good-looking lover who will have the capability of keeping her interest in life.

FLEAS. There is no good omen of dreaming of having been bitten by fleas. It predicts that one will be slandered by those whom he or she believed to be friends. An inconstant lover is suggested by a dream of seeing fleas on the person you love.

FLIGHT. A young woman who dreams of fleeing from any adversary or condition should look to her actions, for if she does not take care to avoid criticism, she may be jilted by her lover.

FLOOD. Any dream of flood is a portent of disaster in business or in love whether in the married state or not.

FLUTE. For unmarried people to dream of playing a flute is a prediction that they will fall in love chiefly on account of the manners of the object of their affections and not particularly for their sterling qualities.

FLYING. Dreams of flying are usually dreams of good omen. Success in love is foretold to those who have pleasant dreams of this kind, as, for instance, soaring easily above country that is green and fertile. A repetition of this dream is particularly lucky.

To dream of flying over desert land, or to fly with difficulty, is a sign that the dreamer will have many obstacles to overcome although he or she will eventually be successful.

FOOT LOG. A woman who dreams of crossing a clear stream of water on a foot log may look forward to having a husband who will treat her with the utmost consideration. But if the water she crosses is muddy, her husband will be difficult to get along with.

If a widow dreams of falling from a foot log into clear water, she has every reason to expect another suitable mate will soon appear with happy results.

FOREHEAD. A maiden who dreams of kissing her lover's forehead should look to her actions because the chances are that her lover will have reason to criticize her for indiscreet conduct.

FORK. A married woman dreaming of a fork or forks is likely to be unhappy. Lovers having this dream will be separated.

FORSAKING. Difficulties in love affairs will follow a dream of a maiden forsaking her home.

If she dreams of forsaking a friend, she will find that as time passes her lover will be less attractive to her.

FORTUNE TELLING. A young woman dreaming of having her fortune told will have to choose shortly between two rivals for her hand.

FOUNTAIN. A married woman who sees a leaping

fountain in the moonlight is liable to be deserted by her lover.

**FRECKLES.** One or more freckles seen in a mirror by a young married woman is a portent of her losing her lover through the conspiracy of one she considered her friend.

**FROGS.** A bullfrog seen by a woman in a dream is a prognostication of marriage with a rich widower who has several children.

**FROGS' LEGS.** A dream of eating frogs' legs is an indication of an inheritance and the pleasant culmination of a love affair from a source that has been hitherto unknown to you.

**FROST.** Frost seen on a window is a sign that the affections of your lover are on the wane.
   Seen on the ground indicates a quick termination of your love affair.

**FRUIT.** *Eating* fruit in a dream is a warning of a degrading experience and consequent unhappiness in love.
   *Seeing* ripe fruit on a tree is a happy augury for both men and women in love.
   *Buying and selling* fruit is an indication of an active but unsuccessful courtship.

**FUNERAL.** An unhappy marriage and unhealthy children are predicted by a dream of seeing a funeral.
   A woman who dreams of wearing black to a funeral is likely to have an early widowhood.

**FURS.** Furs are lucky in dreams. To see them predicts wealth and honor and for a maiden to dream that she is wearing expensive furs further denotes that her husband will be a man of great wisdom.

# G

**GARBAGE.** This is not a good dream for women for it

predicts desertion by their lovers or family troubles.

GARDEN. The happiest kind of a life and an income sufficient for all one's needs is indicated where there is a dream of walking through a lovely garden with one's lover.

GARLIC. An improvement in both your financial and love affairs is presaged by a dream of walking through a garlic patch.

A young woman who dreams of eating garlic will make a marriage based on money considerations rather than love.

GARTER. A maiden who dreams of losing her garter is in danger of having her lover jealous and suspicious of a better looking and wealthier man.

A married man who dreams of a garter should watch his step. It is an omen of keeping company with light and frivolous persons.

A young woman who dreams that her lover fastens a garter on her will keep his affection and belief through all derogatory criticisms.

GAUZE. For a man to see his lady love wearing a dress made of gauze or other very light material is a sign that he will be able to influence her in most of their plans.

GEESE. A man who dreams of geese is assured of the worthiness of the one he loves.

GEMS. To dream of real gems is a good sign in financial and love affairs. If the gems are imitation, or in bad condition, or in unusual surroundings, ill luck is likely to follow.

GIFTS. For an unmarried woman to dream that she is given expensive and beautiful gifts is a sign that her marriage will be a fortunate one both in worldly goods and in happiness.

**GLASS, LOOKING.** (*See* Mirror). To see your reflection in a looking-glass means that you will be neglected in marriage and you will have bad luck in financial affairs.

If a woman sees her lover in a looking-glass, it is a sign that she will have grounds for a breach-of-promise suit.

A married woman seeing her husband in a mirror may look forward to anxiety through his possible dishonesty.

It is a warning against coming indiscretions if a woman sees the reflection of a man other than her husband in the looking-glass.

For a man to see the reflection of women he does not know means that he should guard against entangling alliances.

**GLEANING.** Marriage with a stranger is foretold by a woman who is working among gleaners in a wheat field.

**GLOVES.** Either a marriage or a new love affair is denoted by finding a pair of gloves. If the gloves are in good condition or entirely new, the omen is much better than if they are old and worn.

Misfortune in love or business is the portent of a dream wherein one pulls off his or her gloves.

**GOAT.** If a maiden dreams of drinking goat's milk, it is a sign that she will marry for money and that she will be successful in finding at the same time the man she loves.

**GOBLET.** If a woman dreams of giving a man a goblet of water, it is a sign of unholy pleasures ahead. If she gives him a goblet of wine, it is a prediction of a situation wherein only one's best judgment can avoid disaster.

**GOLD.** A woman who dreams of receiving presents of gold in any form will marry a man who is very wealthy but who makes money his chief end in life.

A man dreaming of gold will be the recipient of honor, wealth and love.

**GRASS** (*See* Hay). A dream of well-kept, luxuriant grass in mellow sunshine predicts to lovers much happiness throughout their courtship and marriage.

If the grass is not in good condition and is parched and full of weeds, the reverse may be expected.

GRAVE. This is a dream that foreshadows disappointment in love. It is a presage of the early ending of a love affair and should be regarded as a warning against criticism or any action which may cause jealousy.

GUITAR. If you are playing a guitar in a dream, it predicts that you will be happy with the person you love. It also predicts that by constant effort to make your lover happy you are building for a serene and secure future.

A broken, unstrung, or out of tune instrument portends disappointments in love.

If a young woman dreamer hears a guitar being played, she should be on guard against the fascinations of untoward pleasures and diversions.

A man having this dream will be pursued by women of no character.

GUN. If a woman dreams of shooting at a target, it is a sign that she will be involved in sensational escapades. Such escapades are likely to be connected with jealousy and so this dream should be regarded as a warning against suspicion.

GYPSY. A headlong love affair leading to an unhappy marriage is the result predicted from dreaming of having one's fortune told by a gypsy.

## H

HAGGARD. If one sees a haggard face in a dream, it is a forerunner of defeat in matters pertaining to the heart.

HAIL. A young woman who dreams of watching a hailstorm will be likely to have many difficulties; but if the hail stones are falling while the sun is shining, it is a sign that true love will come after many apparent failures.

**HAIR.** The man who dreams of seeing a golden-haired girl will be successful in winning the love of a woman of the highest type.

A man who dreams that his sweetheart has red hair will be charged with unfaithfulness by the woman he loves.

A married woman who in combing her hair finds that it is snarled and has difficulty in making it stay put, is in danger of losing her husband through flares of ungovernable temper.

A maiden who dreams of women with gray hair will have rivals for the affections of her sweetheart.

If in a dream a man caresses a woman's hair, it is a sign that although the world may condemn him, he will bask in the love and confidence of the woman he wishes to marry.

If a young woman dreams that her hair turns white over night while her face remains young, will lose her sweetheart suddenly either by illness or some catastrophe.

**HALTER.** A man or woman who dreams of putting a halter on a colt will find that their love affairs will move smoothly and there will be no difficulties encountered before marriage.

**HANDS.** If a woman admires her own hands in a dream, it is an omen that she will win the love of the man she admires more than any other.

Admiration of another's hands mean that a woman will be subject to jealousy of the man she loves.

If she dreams of having a man hold her hands she should regard it as a warning against indiscretions. If she allows a man to kiss her hands she will be gossiped about by those she considered her friends.

**HANDKERCHIEFS.** A dream of clean handkerchiefs indicates the probability of a violent flirtation with someone you have not yet met.

If the handkerchiefs are wrinkled or soiled, it is an

omen of disquieting news from an absent lover.

The loss of a handkerchief foretells that your engagement will be broken for some reason over which you have no control.

To see torn handkerchiefs is a presage of a quarrel with your lover which will probably not be adjusted satisfactorily.

HAREM. If a woman dreams that she is in the harem of an eastern potentate, it does not augur well for her behavior in the near future. She should regard this as a warning against intrigue or careless associations.

To dream that she is the favorite in a harem predicts that she will be pursued by many men of light and frivolous character.

HARLEQUIN. For a man to dream that he is dressed as a harlequin is a warning that designing and mercenary women will lure him to sinful paths.

HARP. A broken engagement is signified by dreaming of a harp that is unstrung or otherwise in bad condition.

If one dreams of playing a harp, it is a sign that his or her nature is too trusting and that one should beware of showing too much confidence in those with whom he or she believes himself in love.

HASH. A woman who dreams that she is cooking hash should beware of yielding to fits of jealousy whether of her husband or her friends or relatives.

To dream of eating hash is a forerunner of a visit from someone whom you know very slightly and whom you have not seen for many years.

HATRED. The man or woman who dreams of hating a person of the opposite sex will find that a love affair will develop before long.

HAY (*See* Grass). A thriving field of hay before it is cut indicates a calm, peaceful married life.

A hay field in which the hay has been cut and stacked

into haycocks indicates that a favorite project will be successfully completed or that a love affair will culminate in marriage.

HEDGES. Strolling along a hedgerow with a person of the opposite sex is an indication of a happy outcome of a problem that may be vexing you, especially in love affairs.

If the hedge seems to be an obstruction of progress, lovers may expect quarrels or other events that will stand in the way of their marriage.

HEELS (*See* Soles). Wearing very high heels in a dream presages being considerably upset by the attentions of one of the opposite sex.

To have a heel come off while you are walking is an indication that you will have some excellent luck within a short time, particularly if the heel is not lost but is fastened on the shoe very shortly afterward.

To catch the heel in a hole or iron grating is a sign that you will be thwarted in some plan that you have made.

To dream that you wear shoes with very low heels is an indication that carelessness will be likely to cause you difficulties which you will find hard to overcome.

HIPS. If a man dreams of admiring voluptuous hips, he will be upbraided by his wife or sweetheart for some fancied wrong.

A maiden who dreams of being satisfied with her hips may expect to be disappointed by her lover.

HOE. Hoeing in a dream presages the ability to carve out one's destiny in both business and love.

HOMINY. A strange dream that has in it an omen of pleasure from dalliance with the opposite sex as a relaxation from important and confining labors. There is no particular significance as to the morality of this dream. Its implications are for both sexes, whether married or single.

103

**HONEY.** Eating honey is a prediction of the early realization of the joys of married life; or for married people a straightening out of difficulties with their in-laws.

**HONEYSUCKLE.** The sight or scent of honeysuckle is good luck in every way to those who have romantic attachments, either inside or outside matrimony.

**HOOD.** A young woman who dreams of wearing a hood is likely to use her wiles to tempt a man to leave the straight and narrow path.

**HORN.** A man who blows a horn of any kind in a dream is in danger of making himself ridiculous through trying to achieve some impossible object.

A maiden who has this dream will eventually realize that she is more impatient to be married than is the man on whom her love is centered.

**HORSE.** (*See* Mare). Dreaming of a black horse is unlucky for a married woman as it denotes unfaithfulness on the part of her husband.

Brood mares indicate companionship and connubial happiness.

Being kicked by a horse is a sign that the object of your affection will do something to make you realize that you have made a mistake.

Having a horse shod is a good omen for lovers, both married and single.

To see one or more horses drawing a cart foretells wealth, but accompanied by distress, especially to lovers.

**HOUNDS.** A dream of hounds is a prediction that a woman will marry a man of low degree, while for a man it predicts an increase in his fortune.

**HUGGING.** This dream foretells disappointment in love if it is not complicated by a situation in which a maiden finds herself hugging a strange man or a married woman hugging a man other than her husband. In the latter cases it is an omen of disgrace through ill-advised actions.

HUNGER. An unhappy and childless marriage is indicated if lovers dream that they are hungry.

HUSBAND. If a woman's husband seems to be leaving her, it is a sign that quarrels will ensue, but the chances are that through some unusual circumstance there will be a reconciliation and a happy outcome.

HYENA. Misunderstandings of a serious nature will follow this dream by lovers or husband and wife.

# I

ICE. IF you dream of ice, it is a sign that your best beloved will do something particularly nice for you.

Hearing the clink of ice in a tumbler or pitcher is an indication that some pressing problem will be solved to your entire satisfaction.

ICE CREAM. Enjoying ice cream in a dream is a propitious sign in all matters pertaining to the heart, but it is a forerunner of sorrow and disillusionment if you upset a dish of ice cream or if it is sour, salty or without flavor.

A dish of ice cream that is almost entirely melted foretells the frustration of one's dearest hopes.

IMAGES. Images or small statues are a harbinger of the termination of a love affair.

A broken image portends a broken vow and is a very unlucky dream.

INCANTATION. Hearing incantations has an unfortunate significance. It means quarrels to come between lovers or inside families.

If you dream that you are yourself repeating incantations for some ulterior purpose, it betokens an opportunity that you will have for an underhanded act which will bring you temporary success.

**INDIFFERENCE.** A dream of indifference on the part of a maiden shows that her sweetheart is not worthy of her.

If she dreams that she is indifferent to him, it is a portent that she will have a new lover before the month is out.

**INDIGO.** To see water with the color of indigo is a sign that you must exercise great circumspection so that you will not be involved in a love affair that will cause scandalous tongues to wag.

**INFIRMITIES.** Your love will fail to live up to your estimate of him or her if you dream of people afflicted with infirmities. These may include people who are injured, disfigured, hunchbacks or who have legs or arms missing.

**INSOLVENT.** To dream that other people than yourself are insolvent or bankrupt means that a young woman will have a lover who will be honest and of a saving disposition, although it is not a good augury for a happy married life.

**INTEMPERANCE** (*See* Drunkenness). A dream of intemperance in any form, whether in love, liquor or loose living, foretells that lovers will be separated through a quarrel that cannot be patched up.

**IRONING** (*See* Washer-woman). To dream that you burn your hands while ironing is a forerunner of unhappiness through jealousy.

One who scorches the clothes she is ironing will have a rival for her sweetheart, thereby causing her considerable worry.

Trying to work with a cold iron indicates to a woman that there will be a lack of affection within her home.

**ISLAND.** For a maiden to dream that she is resting comfortably on a small island surrounded by clear, limpid water predicts a happy marriage with the man of her choice.

IVY. A young woman who dreams of ivy on a castle wall may look forward to an exciting love affair with a romantic young man.

If this dream is of a moonlight scene, it augurs a clandestine meeting with a man of unsavory reputation.

If the ivy is withered, it points to a broken engagement.

## J

JAIL. The young woman who dreams that her lover is in jail is forewarned of the underlying weaknesses in his moral make-up which have hitherto remained concealed.

JASPER. A person who sees jasper in a dream has exceedingly favorable prospects. His or her deepest affections will be ardently returned. An equally bright outlook in money affairs looms for the one who dreams of this stone.

The young woman who loses a jasper may do well to avoid crossing her lover in any important matter, for a disagreement of a serious nature may erect a barrier between them.

JEALOUSY. If in a dream a man finds himself jealous of his wife, he should investigate the origin of a plot hatched by conniving persons with whom he has had business and social dealings.

If he is jealous of a sweetheart, he will find himself entangled in a controversy with a rival. There is success for him in his love if he can keep his temper.

For a woman to dream that she is jealous of her husband indicates a period of inharmonious relationship brought about by a thoughtless deed.

A young woman who dreams that she is jealous of her lover will jump at a rash conclusion as to the intensity of his devotion.

If a person of either sex experiences jealousy in a dream, he or she will suffer from undeserved insults that will disturb the usually smooth course of their relations.

JEWELS. The young unmarried woman who dreams that she is given jewels will rejoice in a life of complete satisfaction. Her desire for luxury will be gratified through a marriage with a person of high character and good business qualities.

If she dreams that she loses valuable jewels, she will have a highly dramatic affair of the heart with the proverbial happy ending. (Separate jewels are found under their proper headings).

JEW'S-HARP. One who plays a jew's harp while dreaming will travel extensively and find a sincere admirer of another nationality.

JIG. If you see your sweetheart dancing a jig in a dream, you may know that his or her temperament is sufficiently buoyant to carry you through a period of long depression of spirit.

JOCKEY. A young woman who dreams of having a jockey for a companion, or sweetheart, will be taken advantage of in a love affair by tricky dealings.

JUBILEE. It is a good sign for a young woman to dream of a jubilee, for it denotes a joyful celebration in connection with her marriage to a prosperous and genial young man.

JUMPING. If you jump down from a wall in a dream, you will rush headlong into an unwise business venture and live to regret your impulsive actions in a love affair.

JUNIPER. A person of either sex whose love affairs have caused disappointment or grief may look forward to a happy solution of his or her problems.

**KATYDID.** A maiden who hears katydids in her dreams is in danger of losing her love through a vacillating attitude toward him.

To see them means that he will prove industrious and moderately successful but an irritating person to live with.

**KETTLE.** Bright kettles presage a rosy fortune while dark kettles are an omen of unhappiness.

A copper kettle is an augury of quiet domestic bliss.

An aluminum kettle foretells a love affair which will move so smoothly that it will seem too good to be true.

An iron kettle denotes happiness through health and love but without more than enough money to supply the necessities of life.

A tin kettle foretells a change in matrimonial affairs either for better or for worse.

A kettle that sings as it boils is a sign of happiness with your mate.

A kettle that boils dry is a portent of disaster in relation to your sweetheart.

**KEY.** To dream of losing a key, means the loss of a lover after a quarrel which has little chance of being made up.

Unlocking a door betokens the advent of a new lover who will not live up to the confidence you repose in him or her.

Locking a door is an omen of good judgment in the selection of a husband or wife.

**KIDNAPING.** To dream that you are implicated in the kidnaping of either a child or a grown person, is an indication that you should exercise extreme caution in making friends among the opposite sex. This dream is not necessarily unlucky, but it is a warning which should be taken carefully into account.

If you are kidnaped or taken away against your will, the omen is of an important development with regard to your future, particularly in matters pertaining to the grand passion.

KIDNEY. To dream of eating kidney stew, or kidneys cooked by another method, is a portent of criticism from some low-minded individual who has found out about your love affairs.

KING. For a young woman to find herself in the presence of a king means that she will be afraid of the man she marries, or if she is already married, she will fear her husband.

If she receives a gift or other special courtesies from a king, she may look forward to a happy marriage.

KISS. To kiss your lover in the dark is a sign of danger ahead; therefore, after such a dream one should be particularly careful to avoid the semblance of indiscreet actions.

Honorable intentions are signified where a man dreams of kissing his sweetheart where it is light.

For a man to kiss a strange woman foretells a sagging moral code.

For married people to dream of kissing each other is a forerunner of harmony in home life.

If a young woman dreams of seeing her sweetheart kissing another woman, it is a sign that her plans for marriage will come to naught.

For a man to dream of his rival kissing his sweetheart portends danger of losing her.

A false friend is likely to exercise spite if a young woman dreams that she is seen kissing her lover.

No good may be expected from a dream of kissing a person of the opposite sex on the neck.

KITCHEN. A spick and span kitchen seen in a dream predicts to a maiden that she will be happily married and take great pleasure in her home life.

A man having this dream is assured of a wife who will be an excellent housekeeper and a perfect mother.

**KITE.** A maiden who dreams of making a kite must look to her methods of winning a suitable husband, for she will be inclined to misrepresent her station in life and will be likely to deceive in small matters.

**KNEES.** Many admirers but no proposals are predicted to a woman who dreams that she has beautiful knees.

**KNIFE.** A separation of lovers is foretold by dreaming of a large knife. If the knife is rusty, the separation will be attended with heartbreak or disgrace on the part of either.

To see meat of any kind being cut with a knife, is an augury that some serious difficulty will be helped by heroic treatment.

**KNIFE GRINDER.** Misfortune in marriage, or hard labor are predicted by a dream of seeing a knife grinder at work.

**KNITTING.** An ideal home with a charming mate and several lovely children may be confidently expected by a woman who dreams of knitting.

If a young woman dreams that she has a job in a knitting mill, it signifies that she will suddenly find the man of her choice and will marry him in a very short time with every probability of happiness.

**KNOTS.** Vexations over matters of small importance will occur if you dream of seeing knots in string or cord. You will be jealous if your sweetheart even notices another.

Tying a knot is a sign that you will be independent and self-assertive, both of which qualities you should avoid over-emphasizing.

Untying a knot is a forerunner of the solution of a vexing difficulty.

## L

**LABORATORY.** Dreaming of being a chemist in a laboratory means that you will be unsuccessful in business and that the woman you love will prove a great disappointment to you.

If you dream of making a successful experiment that has hitherto eluded you and others, it is a sign of wealth but not a happy culmination of your love affair.

LABYRINTH. A place of winding and intricate passages or a garden labyrinth in which you are lost is an omen of home conditions which are distressing and shameful.

An engaged person should take warning from such a dream, for lovers will be shown up as irritable and without consideration.

LACE. For a man to dream of seeing lace on his sweetheart's garments is a good sign even though it is on the edge of a slip or petticoat which shows beneath the skirt. She will be faithful in love and an excellent mother to your children.

A woman who dreams of lace on her undergarments will be likely to have her wishes fulfilled, particularly in the choice of a handsome and wealthy husband.

A maiden who dreams of making lace will soon meet a good-looking man of excellent future who will ask for her hand in marriage.

If she dreams of trimming her wedding lingerie with lace, she will have many lovers but it will be a long time before she is married.

LAKE. Lovers who dream of a lake which is little more than a mud hole and which has an air of bleakness are likely to find that their love affair will shortly come to an end.

To dream of seeing trees and their leaves reflected in a lake, means that you will soon tire of the person with whom you believe yourself to be in love.

LANTERN. A young woman who has a dream of lighting a lantern held by her lover may look forward to a marriage with a man of good circumstances and charm.

For her to blow out a lantern, is a sign that she will lose an opportunity to marry such a man.

**LAP.** A maiden who dreams of sitting on a man's lap had better watch her step for she will be the target of criticism from jealous and gossipy persons.

**LAUREL.** This is a dream which indicates that you will be fortunate in your love affair as well as in various other enterprises.

To place a wreath of laurel on her sweetheart's head, is a sign that a maiden will shortly be wooed by a man who is handsome, wealthy and charming.

**LAWNS.** Awaiting on a green and well-kept lawn for the coming of a lover is a sign to a young woman that her ambitions regarding marriage with a wealthy man will be realized.

If the lawn is brown, weedy and ill-kept, the reverse may be expected.

**LAZINESS.** A young woman who dreams that her sweetheart is lazy, should look to her actions for they are likely to be such as would discourage men who would otherwise court her seriously.

**LEAD.** It is a sign that your sweetheart will reveal a deceitful and ill-tempered nature if you dream of seeing or entering a lead mine.

**LEAVES.** Those who dream of leaves which are green and tender will inherit a legacy from either a relative or a rich friend and they will make a very advantageous marriage.

**LEAVETAKING** (*See* Forsaking).

**LEDGER** (*See* Accounts). A single woman who dreams of a ledger will have a proposal of marriage from a business man of comfortable means.

**LEGS.** A maiden who dreams of admiring her own legs will,

113

through her vanity, fail to enlist the love of the man whom she admires most.

If she has much hair on her legs, she will be the leader in all family matters.

LENTILS. A young woman dreaming of lentils will try to break an engagement with her affianced, but through the advice of others including her parents she will accept him and probably be sorry.

LEPROSY. To dream of seeing those who are suffering with this frightful disease, is a sign that your lover will gradually sink into indifference.

LETTERS. If you dream of receiving a letter that is delivered by hand, it is an indication that you have done something which is not considered upright by your lover.

A letter written with white ink on a dark paper is an unlucky portent. It indicates separation between husband and wife or between lovers, and it may be accompanied by unwholesome allegations.

A warning that you should beware of unworthy concerns is contained in a dream of trying to hide a letter from your sweetheart, wife, or husband.

A registered letter is a portent of family troubles and selfishness on the part of one or the other of two lovers. Jealousy of a rival is indicated by a registered letter.

A happy letter of an affectionate nature is a pleasant augury; but if it is written on colored paper, it indicates that there will be difficulties in love or in business. Written in blue ink on white paper is a sign that you will be lucky in love and in money matters.

A maiden who dreams of receiving a letter from her lover and placing it close to her heart will have cause to be worried by a beautiful rival.

LIAR. For one to dream of believing that his or her lover has told a lie, is a warning of differences which will not be easy to overcome. It is likely to portend a broken engagement.

**LICENSE.** An automobile license seen in a dream is an omen of meeting a person of the opposite sex who will have an important message for you. This may lead to an engagement and a happy marriage.

**LIGHTNING.** It is bad luck to dream that you are struck by lightning for it is a forerunner of sorrow in love, family, or business affairs.

**LILY.** Illness, disgrace, or death are signified by dreaming of lilies. Those who are engaged to be married will be rendered unhappy following such a dream.

**LIME KILN.** No good is foretold by dreaming of seeing a lime kiln, especially for those who are in love. The chances are much against a happy culmination of the affair.

**LION.** A man who dreams of hearing a lion roar is likely to have the adulation of many beautiful women.

A woman who has this dream will achieve her fondest hopes in being courted by a man of wealth and personality.

A maiden who dreams of young lions will have several intensely interesting lovers before she finally marries the right man.

To dream of seeing a lion trainer putting the animals through their paces, is an indication that the dreamer will have much admiration from the opposite sex and that before long a fortunate marriage will be contracted.

**LIPS.** A man who dreams of lovely, natural, red lips is assured that his love is reciprocated by the object of his affection.

Heavy, sensual lips signify a marriage in which ill temper will mar the happiness of both parties.

**LIZARD.** If a woman dreams that a lizard crawls up her leg, it is an omen that her husband will die and that she will have to work for a living thereafter.

To kill a lizard is a lucky portent, both in love and in business.

**LOAVES.** Loaves of cake are an omen of riches, both in money and in love, unless they are broken.

Loaves of bread signify plenty, but they are not particularly significant of success in love, for they betoken a very matter-of-fact existence.

**LOCK.** For one to dream of locking up one's lover is a sign that suspicion will work harm to the affair; but it also indicates that, after a period of doubt, matters will be satisfactorily cleared up.

Locks in general mean that lovers will come to a happy culmination of their affair after many difficulties.

If one tries unsuccessfully to unlock a door or closet, it is a presage of an unhappy termination of an engagement.

**LOCKET.** A maiden who dreams of having a locket placed around her neck, may confidently expect that she will soon be married and that she will have beautiful children.

If she dreams of losing a locket, she will be saddened by a death in her family or by the death of her lover.

A man who dreams that his sweetheart gives back a locket with which he has presented her, will be harassed by the suspicion of the one he loves.

**LOOM.** A beautiful woman at work on a loom, weaving a pleasing pattern, is a fortunate dream for those who are in love. It means a happy and harmonious married life.

If a woman dreams of weaving, it is a prediction that she will have a handsome husband and two or more beautiful children.

**LOTTERY.** Inconstancy on the part of her husband is indicated to the woman who dreams of buying a lottery ticket. She will be subject to many disappointments because of her husband's indifference.

116

If one dreams of winning a lottery prize, it is a sign that love affairs will be pleasant but productive of no lasting good.

LOVE. This is a dream which foretells happiness in nearly every case. It is especially fortuitous when you dream of being loved by others, and the only time when it is not a good sign is when your love for someone else is not reciprocated.

The love of husband and wife, of parents and children, and of sweethearts is a dream which foretells good fortune, happiness, and wealth.

The love of animals is an indication that you will adjust yourself easily to conditions as they are.

LUGGAGE. A broken engagement is foretold by a dream of luggage of any kind, such as trunks, suit-cases, bags, etc.

LYNX. A rival in love is indicated by a dream of a lynx. If the dreamer kills a lynx, it means that the rival will be put to rout.

LYRE. It is a dream of good portent for young people to play in tune on a lyre, for it signifies that they will have the affection and loyalty of a worthy mate.

If the lyre is unstrung, or out of tune, the reverse may be expected.

# M

MADNESS (*See* Asylum, Insanity). The young woman who dreams of suddenly going mad receives a premonition of coming misfortunes connected with her love affair and her financial state.

MAGNET. A dream of a magnet is an indication to a man that he will be drawn by a woman into unsavory alliances and that he will clear his name finally but with great difficulty.

For a woman to see a magnet in a dream presages a secure, sheltered existence with a thoughtful husband who supplies all her needs.

MARE. (*See* Horse). If a young woman dreams of seeing mares in lush, green pastures, she may expect a marriage without regrets and children who will do credit to her and her husband.

MARMALADE. A season of tantalizing and unsatisfactory domestic life is denoted by a dream of making marmalade or jam.

MARRIAGE. Disappointments in her love affairs are predicted to the young woman who dreams of being married, particularly if the dream is accompanied by no particular thrill or excitement. If she is a happy bride and the dream gives her extreme pleasure, the portent is one which should be comforting to a woman in love.

It is a happy augury to dream of being a bridesmaid, a maid of honor, or a best man at a wedding, for you will have cause to be thankful for the loving attentions of those who are close to you.

To dream of being present at a wedding where all the circumstances are joyful, means happy years ahead. If the guests are dressed in black or dark colors, the dreamer has sorrow to look forward to.

A woman who dreams that she marries a man of advanced years is likely to have much trouble in the near future. It is a portent of illness, bad news and other kinds of ill luck.

MASK. A young woman who dreams of being at a party where masks are worn should beware of unseemly behavior in public.

If she unmasks, it is a sign that through her honesty she will find herself in difficulties through no fault of her own but, nevertheless, her trials will seem serious until they are finally overcome.

MELANCHOLY. It is a sign of separation from the one

you love to dream that you are melancholy or that you see others in the same state.

MELODY (*See* Music.). To dream of hearing a melody is a good sign for everyone. It is an omen to lovers that they will find life's greatest happiness in the marriage which is sure to come within a short time. It foretells harmony in the home life and children who will be a credit to their parents.

MENDING. Success as a wife is predicted to the young woman who dreams of mending.

MILE POST. It is unlucky so far as love affairs are concerned to dream that you see a mile post. To pass one indicates that you will take extraordinary chances without much certainty as to whether or not you will find success.

MILLER. A woman who dreams of a miller grinding corn, wheat, or other cereal, is likely to be deceived in the financial condition of the man who has asked her to be his wife.

MINK. A young woman who dreams of being presented with a mink coat is in danger of being criticized for behavior which, although innocent, may have the semblance of dissoluteness.

To dream of stroking the soft fur of a mink garment, foretells a proposition of some sort that should be weighed carefully before accepting, as it may be compromising.

MIRROR (*See* Glass). A man who dreams of seeing a woman before a dressing table looking in a hand-mirror may be assured that the girl whom he asks to be his wife will accept him, but that she will be vain and capricious.

A woman who dreams of looking at her back with the aid of a hand-mirror will have a proposal within six months from a man whom she has never met before.

To break a mirror in a dream, means that the dream-

119

er will be disappointed in a person he or she has regarded as a friend. It also foretells an unhappy marriage and delicate children.

MISER. One who dreams of a miser counting his money will be disappointed in someone who seemed to be a true friend or lover.

A maiden who dreams that a miser has settled a sum of money on her will have reason to look forward to a whirlwind courtship by a wealthy and handsome young man.

MOCKING BIRD. It is good luck to hear a mocking bird sing, but it is an unfortunate augury in love affairs to see one which is disabled or dead.

MIXING. Any form of mixing is an indication of an upset condition regarding one's relations with the opposite sex.

To dream of mixing cocktails, is a warning that one should use great discretion in any commitments that he or she may be on the point of making.

MODELS. A man who dreams of being in a studio where a female model is posing in the nude will probably realize a pet ambition to which he has been aspiring for a long time.

A young woman who dreams of being a model, whether for an artist, a photographer, or in a dressmaking establishment, is in danger of being involved in a very disquieting love affair.

MONKEY. Dreaming of a monkey, baboon, chimpanzee, or other similar animal, is a sign that a young woman will be charged with unfaithfulness by her lover.

To dream of feeding a monkey peanuts or other food, foretells a betrayal by a person hitherto considered friendly.

MORTGAGE. It is a portent of excellent prospects in love to dream of reading a mortgage, particularly if it seems to be a document in your favor.

MOTOR CAR (See Collision, Skidding). The significance of riding in a motor car depends largely upon the attendant circumstances: whether the car is running smoothly, swiftly, slowly, or otherwise. It also depends on the character of the country through which it is proceeding.

In general the idea of riding means progress in affairs of business or love and the indications mentioned above have their effect upon the dream. If, for instance, a motor is stalled, it is a prediction of difficulties in a project which one is trying to work out. Hilly country, badly paved roads and such difficulties augur a slowing up of the progress but do not mean that the project will not be completed. The comfort of the car is also an indication of the ease with which the end may be attained. A car without good springs, for instance, or one which is in bad mechanical condition, is an augury of difficulty.

MOURNING. To dream of seeing others wearing mourning or to wear it yourself, is an indication of the separation of lovers.

MUFF. A man who dreams of seeing his sweetheart with a muff will have cause to regret it, for it is an augury that someone more capable than himself will take his place as her lover.

MULE. Keen regret in relation to love affairs is foretold by dreaming of being kicked by a mule.

A maiden who dreams of a white mule will marry a man of foreign birth who, although of great wealth, will be difficult to live with.

A maiden dreaming of mules in pastures will for a time have many admirers, but they will not ask her for her hand in marriage.

MUSIC (See Melody). The significance of a dream in which music is heard depends largely upon whether or not it is harmonious. If it is thoroughly pleasing, it foretells calm, happy days in love, matrimony, and business.

121

If the instruments are out of tune, or if there is an occasional sour note in the music, it is a portent of coming trouble.

MUSK. The odor of musk predicts joy through the smoothing out of lovers' difficulties.

MUSTACHE. A woman who dreams of admiring a mustache should be extremely careful of her conduct, for her virtue is in danger.

MYRRH. A young woman who dreams of the odor of myrrh has cause to be excited, for it foretells that she will make a new acquaintance with considerable wealth and the ambition to make her happy.

MYRTLE. A sprig of myrtle worn by a maiden in a dream is an indication to her that she will contract a very favorable marriage with a man of unlimited financial resources and great intelligence.

# N

NAKEDNESS (*See* Nudity). A dream of nakedness in either sex is one which portends disillusionment after an affair of the heart which has been intense though not on a high plane. Nakedness is an omen of highly realistic developments in love affairs and a final coming down to earth to meet a drab existence.

NEARSIGHTEDNESS. For a man to dream that his intended is nearsighted is a portent of a broken engagement.

NECKLACE. It is a fortunate augury for a young woman to dream of receiving a necklace as a gift, for it foretells a husband of character and means, and a happy home life.

NEGRO. A heavy-set and very dark negro is a dream that predicts a rival for the affections of a sweetheart, wife, or husband.

**NIGHTGOWN.** A man who dreams of seeing his intended in a filmy nightgown may be assured of her love for him and her innocent though sensible attitude toward life.

**NIGHTINGALE.** Future happiness and content to lovers is predicted by dreaming that one hears the song of a nightingale.

**NOBILITY.** Any nobility of character that is brought out in a dream is a good sign. It foretells a loving and even-tempered mate.

A maiden who dreams of a member of the nobility, such as a duke, earl, or other, will be impressed by a man dependable in his character.

**NUDITY** (*See* Nakedness). Nudity in dreams has many beautiful implications, whether it is of a man, woman, or child.

For one to dream of admiring his or her own nudity, predicts the loss of a lover through vain ideas; but if a person is disgusted with the appearance of the body, it foretells scandal and lovers' quarrels.

If one dreams of swimming in the nude, it is a prediction of pagan pleasures which will react unfavorably.

To dream of seeing men and women, swimming in the nude, or as members of a nudist colony, is a sign of a new and exciting love affair.

**NUNS.** A woman who dreams of seeing nuns is likely to be permanently separated from her lover or husband.

**NUTS.** Success in love or in married life is the augury of a dream of gathering nuts from a tree.

Eating nuts is a sign of financial prosperity in addition to the foregoing.

**NYMPH.** To see nymphs bathing or disporting themselves in green places, is an indication to a young woman that she will have many pleasures and interesting compan-

123

ions, but she will be careless of her behavior in connection with these.

If she dreams that she is herself a nymph, she must guard her conduct carefully to avoid leading her men friends astray.

# O

OAK. Lovers who dream of oak trees will begin their married life under the most auspicious circumstances, and if in this dream there are acorns visible, it is a prediction of beautiful children.

OBELISK. Quarrels of a serious nature are portended if one dreams of meeting his or her sweetheart under an obelisk, or other tall shaft of stone.

OCEAN. A calm ocean seen in a dream foretells delight to young lovers.

OIL. It is a portent of an unsuccessful love affair if a man dreams that he buys or sells oil.

A woman who dreams that oil is poured upon her head, either as a matter of anointing or in connection with a shampoo of any kind, must beware of advances from a man who has not honorable intentions.

OPULENCE (See Riches).

ORANGES. The loss of her sweetheart is predicted to a maiden who dreams of eating oranges or drinking orange juice.

ORATOR. A dream of a love affair with an orator is an indication that a woman's conduct will be too much governed by the ostentation of her acquaintances.

ORCHARD. Happy homes with fine, upright and well-favored mates are presaged by a dream of walking through an orchard with fruit ripening on the trees.

Men and maidens who dream of meeting in an orchard

124

in blossom are assured of a happy culmination of their fondest desires.

ORCHESTRA. In general it is a pleasant portent to dream of playing an instrument in an orchestra.

If, however, the orchestra plays out of tune, sweethearts will be separated.

ORGANIST. A maiden who dreams that she is playing an organ must beware of being too exacting in her demands upon her lover and should zealously avoid any actions which might indicate that she is jealous.

ORNAMENT. To dream of losing an ornament, particularly in the form of jewelry, predicts the loss of a lover.

OTTER. Both maids and matrons may be confident of the most tender attentions from their sweethearts or husbands if they dream of seeing an otter swimming.

OTTOMAN (See Bed, Bedroom). The earliest possible marriage with your affianced is advised by a dream in which you and your sweetheart sit together upon an ottoman or other low upholstered furniture, for enemies are likely to gossip unkindly about you to your lover.

OVEN. Difficulties are foretold by a dream of a very hot oven, but a woman who has this dream may look forward to the love of her friends and family.

An oven which will not heat sufficiently for baking purposes predicts a misunderstanding with a lover.

OVERALLS. Infidelity is suggested to a woman who dreams of seeing a man in overalls. For her to dream of wearing them herself, portends a future with the man she loves for his sterling character rather than his ability to provide her with luxuries.

OX (See Cattle). A man who dreams of seeing a fine yoke of oxen may look forward to success both as a business man and a lover. He will probably receive more attentions from the gentler sex than he will appreciate.

Lovers' devotion is indicated by a dream of oxen drinking at a pleasant stream of water.

OYSTERS. The buying and selling of oysters is an indication that you must guard the manner of your approach in attempting to win a wife or husband. This applies equally well in the attempt to make a fortune.

# P

PACIFYING (See PEACEMAKING). A dream in which a suitor sees himself attempting to calm his sweetheart and restore her trust in him warns him that petty disagreements will make their union undesirable.

PAGODA. A young woman who dreams that she and her lover enter a pagoda will find that a series of obstacles to their marriage will arise. The combined energies of the lovers will be required to overcome these hindrances. If the pair are alone in the pagoda, it is a prediction that the obstacles will prove too much for them.

PAINT. To paint a picture while dreaming is an indication to a young woman that her sweetheart's affection for her is not strong enough to prevent his becoming infatuated with others.

PALACE (See Buildings, Castle). If a young unmarried woman in straitened circumstances dreams that she attends the festivities in a house of extraordinary beautiful appointments, she will be likely to find favor in the eyes of a person of rank and wealth.

PALM TREES. It is a portent of a joyous home life with a handsome and adoring husband for a maiden to dream of walking through a row of palm trees.

For a man to dream that he sees coconut palms being climbed by black boys is a sign of some unexpected and curious event that will come about through the activities of his sweetheart.

**PALSY.** If a lover should dream that his or her sweetheart has an affliction which causes the limbs to shake, it is a prediction that there will be difficulties of a very disquieting nature, and that only supreme will power will overcome them.

**PANTHER.** To dream of seeing a panther appearing with a suddenness that startles, portends a broken engagement or other disappointment in a love affair.

To dream of killing a panther or outwitting the animal, is a very good sign for lovers.

**PAPER.** To dream of handling paper, is a portent of a quarrel with a lover or within the home. This holds good whether it is wrapping paper, writing paper, or newspaper.

**PARABLES.** A dream of hearing a parable, or a story told to illustrate a point, prophesies to the engaged person that the object of his or her affections will be disloyal in some particular.

**PARADISE.** Although a dream of being in paradise will have many different qualities according to the person who has the dream, it carries with it a promise of great happiness to lovers and excellent good fortune.

**PARALYSIS.** If a person who is in love dreams that he or she is paralyzed, or that the object of his or her affections is so afflicted, it is a portent that these affections will soon fade away.

**PARASOL.** A parasol, either open or closed, denotes illicit enjoyment and giddy pleasures whether for those who are married or engaged.

**PARENTS** (*See* Mother, Father). A maiden who dreams of either or both of her parents may look forward to a happy marriage with a man of ample means.

**PARK.** A comfortable and happy marriage is foretold by a dream of strolling through a beautiful park.

If there are one or more fountains playing in the sunshine, it is an augury of several well favored children.

**PARKING.** Parking an automobile with ease indicates a solution of difficulties in love and business.

If in a dream one finds difficulties in parking a car, the portent is of a message from a long distance that will hamper an existing or future love affair.

**PARROT.** A maiden dreaming of sitting alone with a parrot should make up her mind that she will have a life of single blessedness.

If a man dreams of hearing a parrot talk, it is a sign that he will find his mate in unusual circumstances.

**PARSNIPS.** Nothing but gloom is ahead for a lover who dreams of seeing or eating parsnips.

**PARTING** (*See* Forsaking).

**PATCH.** For a young man or a young woman to dream of discovering patches in their clothes is a portent that they will have difficulty in hiding something from a lover.

A woman who dreams of patching clothing for some other member of the family may look forward to happiness in the married life but there will be the necessity for conservation of financial resources.

**PAWNSHOP.** When a person dreams of pawning any article it is a sign that he or she will have quarrels with a sweetheart or misfortune in business.

**PEACHES** (*See* Fruit, Orchard). A woman who dreams of gathering ripe and beautiful peaches in an orchard will be likely to travel widely with her husband.

A maiden who has this dream will have the charm and beauty to win a husband of great wealth, taste, and education.

**PEACEMAKING** (*See* Pacifying). A man who dreams of trying to make peace between another man and his wife who are quarreling should be warned of similar quarrels with his own wife, if he marries the girl to whom he is engaged.

**PEARLS.** To dream of receiving a gift of a pearl necklace, is lucky for a maiden for it denotes a peaceful and happy life with a man who will be careful of her every wish.

A man dreaming that he is the giver of pearls should be warned of the vanity of his ladylove.

The loss of pearls is a portent of the loss of love and financial reverses.

**PEARS** (*See* Fruit, Orchard). To dream of cooking pears is an indication that the love affair that you are now engaged in will turn out in a disappointing manner.

**PECANS.** If one dreams of opening pecan nuts and eating them, and one of them is decayed or shriveled, it foretells failure in a love affair.

**PENCIL.** If a young woman should be given a pencil in a dream and should recognize the giver, she will do well to avoid that person's company because no friendship can exist between them.

A maiden who writes a note while dreaming will have a most desirable lover. If the point of the pencil breaks as she writes, she must look to some future sudden parting with her sweetheart.

Should she dream that she erases the words, there is an indication that her love affair will be one that she wishes to forget.

A young man who sees himself in a dream writing large letters with a heavy, black lead pencil will find an easy path to a successful love affair and a fortunate business career.

**PEPPER.** A talented mate will soon be found by the one who sees in a dream sturdy bushes of green peppers growing.

**PETTICOAT.** A taffeta petticoat that rustles beneath a young woman's dress is a sign that the wearer's forward nature will be damaging to her love affair.

If a young woman sees herself in a dream with her petticoat showing beneath her dress, she will regret an unfortunate act of hers which will turn her lover away from her.

For a young man to dream of a petticoat is a warning that his attitude toward the opposite sex should be more courteous or he may ruin his chances with the girl he loves.

**PETTING** (*See* Porch). A maiden who dreams of nestling in the arms of a man she does not know will find that she will shortly be strenuously wooed by one whom she had never previously regarded as a possibility for a lover.

Petting dreams, under circumstances that may be regarded as suitable, are always omens of excellent luck in matters pertaining to the heart.

A man who dreams of having each arm around a different girl should beware of careless proposals.

**PHOSPHORUS.** A young woman who has a dream of gleaming phosphorescent water will find that she has a strong attraction for members of the opposite sex.

**PHOTOGRAPHY.** To dream that you are taking photographs out-of-doors of a person of the opposite sex, is a sign that you will be disappointed in the behavior of someone you love.

Taking motion pictures in a dream predicts that any love affair in which you are at present interested will come to a happy culmination.

**PIANO.** For a person who is unskilled in music to dream of playing the piano successfully is an indication that he or she will win the love of someone who has hitherto appeared indifferent.

If the dream is of an unsuccessful attempt to play the

piano, resulting in a jumble of tuneless sounds, it is an ill omen for lovers.

PICKLES. Very sour pickles augur quarrels between lovers. Sweet pickles foretell serious rivals for the person with whom one has been keeping company.

PICNIC (*See* Party). There is a pleasant future for the maiden who dreams of being at a picnic with her lover, unless rain or other disquieting incidents occur, in which case the opposite may be expected.

PIES (*See* Baker, Baking). A young woman will be flirtatious and too much inclined to lightheartedness in the company of men if she dreams of making pies of any kind.

PIGEONS. A flock of pigeons on the wing or at rest is a harbinger of a placid existence with a harmonious mate. To hear the cooing of pigeons foretells that your mate will be easy to get along with.

PIGS. If one dreams of looking into a pig sty and seeing several porkers wallowing, it is a sign that you will be subject to extreme jealousy on the part of someone of the opposite sex. Greed is also indicated by this dream.

PILLOW. A maiden who dreams of pillows is sure to have a wealthy suitor.
 If she dreams that she is making a pillow, it is a sign of success in her friendships with men.

PINS. A dream of pins, whether of the ordinary variety, hair pins, or safety pins, is a warning to a maiden that she should observe more ladylike conventions toward her sweetheart.

PIRATE. A man who dreams of being a pirate will be accepted by the next woman to whom he proposes.
 If a maiden dreams that her sweetheart is a pirate, she

should go very slowly until he has proved himself worthy of her affections.

PLAGUE. A dream of a plague, pestilence, or epidemic, is a forerunner of almost insurmountable difficulties with one's wife, husband, or lover.

PLANK (*See* Foot Log). Anyone who dreams of crossing a stream or other barrier upon a plank should be exceedingly careful of his or her conduct. The dream is complicated according to the soundness of the plank and its width. If the plank wobbles, or is otherwise insecure, the indications for trouble are that much more positive.

PLATES (*See* Crockery, Dishes). Plates seen in a dream are indications to the unmarried that the dreamer will have a happy and inspiring love affair and a harbinger of happiness to married people.

PLAY (*See* Actor, Singer, Stage). To dream of being at the theatre and watching a play being enacted, either by living people or on the screen, is either lucky or unlucky according to the character of the play. It presages meetings with interesting people of the opposite sex which may lead in almost any direction depending on whether the play is pleasing or harrowing, exciting or dull. One should refer to the subject under its proper heading.

PLOW. If a maiden sees her lover plowing, either with horses or a tractor, it foretells her marriage with a man of stable character and excellent financial prospects.

POCKETBOOK (*See* Purse).

POKER (*See* Cards). Beware of your associations with people of the opposite sex if you dream of playing poker. It is particularly unpropitious if you appear to be winning.

POMEGRANATE. Only a man's strength of character will

save him from being lured into unseemly conduct by a woman's wiles if he dreams that his sweetheart gives him a pomegranate.

A woman who eats a pomegranate is in grave danger of losing her head to some unworthy, though picturesque man.

POOL. Peace and contentment are predicted by dreaming of a limpid pool bordered by flags and containing lilies.

A bathing pool in which men and women are swimming is a sign of news from a long forgotten lover.

POPLARS. A maiden who dreams of standing with her lover beside a poplar tree swaying in a summer breeze is assured of realizing her fondest hopes for a lover who is rich, handsome and true.

Poplars which have shed their leaves bode no good to those who are in love.

PORCH (See Petting). To dream of sitting on a dark porch in summer with a young person of the opposite sex is a sign that there will be a mystery in your life that may take years to solve.

PORCUPINE. For a man or a maid to dream of being hurt by the quill of a porcupine is an augury of discontent and the wish to end a love affair.

POTTER'S FIELD. A young man or woman who dreams of his or her beloved in a potter's field is warned of a coming temptation to transfer love to someone of greater wealth but less breeding and charm.

POTTERY (See Crockery, Dishes, etc.).

PRESSING (See ironing).

PRIEST (See Clergyman, Vicar). It is bad luck for a woman to dream that she is in love with a priest, for it portends the loss of her sweetheart through indiscreet behavior.

**PRINTER.** A woman who dreams of being in love with a printer is almost sure to have trouble with her family.

A man who dreams of being in a printing shop may expect surprising revelations regarding the person he loves best.

**PRINTING SHOP.** If a maiden dreams that her lover works in a printing shop, she will marry a man of good impulses but little financial stability.

**PRIVACY.** To dream of intruding on anyone's privacy, especially of entering a bedroom or bathroom without first receiving permission to do so, presages a serious misunderstanding with lover, husband, or wife.

**PROFANITY.** To dream of being profane signifies embarrassment.

**PROSTITUTE** (*See* Harlot, Vice). A girl who dreams of prostitutes who appear brazen and prosperous should guard her chastity well when among new acquaintances.

If in the dream it should appear that a prostitute is repentant, it is a sign that the dreamer will win a true sweetheart through understanding.

**PUDDING.** A maiden who dreams of making a pudding is in danger of finding that her lover is worldly minded and inclined to woo her for her money.

**PUMP.** A pump with a broken handle is a sign of hope deferred and a blasted love affair.

To dream of easily pumping water, foretells success in love and business.

**PURSE.** To dream of a well-filled purse, shows that fortunes are on the mend, not alone in worldly goods but in spiritual values and love affairs.

To dream that a purse is empty, foretells a disappointment in the person to whom you are engaged.

**PURSUIT.** If you dream of being pursued by a person or an animal, it augurs ill for your future.

Pursuit by an officer of the law, either on foot or mounted on a horse or motorcycle, is an indication that something you would wish hidden will be revealed to your sweetheart.

PYRAMID. Climbing one of the Egyptian pyramids is a portent of an early but unsuccessful marriage.

## Q

QUICKSAND. A dream of being slowly engulfed in quicksand is a portent of difficulties which can be overcome only by heroic treatment. It foretells quarrels with a lover, or with someone you esteem highly.

If a maiden dreams of being rescued by her sweetheart from quicksand, it predicts an early marriage with a man who will be praiseworthy in everything he does.

QUILL. A young woman who in a dream puts a quill or other feathers upon a hat will find that her love affairs will increase in frequency but that she will, in spite of this, be likely to remain a maiden.

QUILTS. Clean, fluffy quilts are a fortunate dream to a young woman as they foretell an easy life with a husband who will give her the things for which she longs.

If the quilts are soiled or worn, her husband will be careless in his treatment of her.

QUADRUPLETS *(See* Twins, Triplets, Quintuplets). Dreaming of quadruplets, whether born to the dreamer or to someone else, is a sign that a love affair is in the offing and will be rushed to a quick culmination.

QUINTUPLETS *(See* Twins, Triplets, Quadruplets). Good luck is foretold by a dream of five children being born at the same time, but if one or more are born dead, it signifies early widowhood for a woman or divorce for a man.

**RABBIT.** A dream of many white rabbits is a sign that your married life will be full of joy and that you will have many children.

**RADIO.** There is no particular significance to hearing a radio in a dream. Any portent that is implied is in the character of the program which is being broadcast. Refer to the subject under its proper heading.

**RAGE.** Unmarried persons who dream of seeing their sweethearts in a rage are likely to have quarrels over some trivial point.

**RAILING.** Railings of any kind, whether used as fences or as guards for porches, stairways, or other places, indicate that there is a rival in the offing for the object of your affections.

To dream of grasping a railing is a prediction that you will take desperate chances to win the person you love.

**RAIN.** If you dream of sitting indoors and watching a violent rain storm outside, it is a sign that your love will be requited.

**RAINBOW.** Happiness for lovers is foretold by a dream in which a rainbow figures.

**RAMROD.** A ramrod denotes the loss of a lover through his or her attention to criticism within the family.

**RATTLE.** A marriage and children are foretold to the young woman who dreams of seeing a baby play with a rattle.

There is a similar portent if a man has this dream.

**RAVEN** (*See* Birds, Crow). A raven in a dream denotes a future in love affairs as black as the raven itself. It indicates betrayal and deception.

**RELIGION** (*See* Church). Dreams of a religious quality should be interpreted according to the items which appear in the dream rather than the emotional side of religion. Thus the meaning of the dream should be ascertained through such references as church, minister, altar, congregation, etc.

**REPRIEVE.** A maiden who dreams that her lover is reprieved on the eve of his execution may reasonably expect to hear shortly of some good luck which has befallen him.

**REPTILE** (*See* Asp, Snake). Treachery through a rival for the hand of a sweetheart is indicated to those who dream of seeing a reptile of one kind or another.

To dream of being bitten by any reptilian animal, means that the rival will be successful.

**RESTAURANT.** To dream of eating in a restaurant with a sweetheart is a sign of coming happiness.

Eating at a lunch counter predicts irritations arising from misunderstanding.

**REVELATION.** To have a secret revealed to you in a dream is a portent of a surprising announcement from your lover. A pleasing revelation is an augury of success but a gloomy one portends failure.

**REVOLVER** (*See* Cartridge, Cannon, Gun). A maiden who dreams that she sees her lover with a revolver, either merely holding it or shooting it, is likely to terminate her present love affair.

**RIBBON.** A woman who dreams of putting ribbons on her dress or on her underwear will shortly have an offer of marriage from a serious-minded young man. But for her to dream of seeing other women wearing ribbons means that she will have difficulties in securing a husband on account of the rivalry of one whom she considered her friend.

137

**RICHES.** Dreams of riches with unbounded luxury are unfortunate alike for men and women for they predict loss of friends or lovers and probable poverty.

**RING.** It is a fortunate dream for a young woman to be given a ring. It predicts that her lover will be faithful and that her married life will be happy.

To dream of a broken ring, predicts quarrels, sickness and other unhappiness.

**RIVAL.** A dream of having a rival is one which should be taken seriously by those who are in love. It is a warning not to be too critical of the one you intend to make your mate.

**ROAD.** A road bordered with green arching trees and pleasant fields is an indication of a thoroughly happy home life with a faithful and interesting mate and several merry children.

**ROCKET.** A rocket soaring into the evening sky is a dream of success in business and love.

**ROCKING CHAIR.** It is a harbinger of happiness, health and plenty to dream of seeing a mother, wife or sweetheart in a rocking chair.

**ROGUE.** If a woman dreams that her husband or lover is a rogue, it is a portent of a temptation that he will have to resist if there is to be happiness in their lives.

**ROOF.** It is a fortunate dream of lovers to find themselves on a roof.

If one dreams of falling off a roof, a change may be expected in their life plans.

**ROPES.** Love-making will be considerably upset if one dreams of tangled ropes.

Neatly coiled rope indicates one's ability to smooth out any difficulties that may arise.

**ROSES.** If roses are blooming on the bush or they are fresh cut in a vase, the predictions are all joyful for those who are in love. They point toward an early marriage and a wide circle of true friends.

**ROUGE.** To dream of applying rouge in a public place is a prediction of a humiliating experience with the object of your affections.

**ROWBOAT.** Those who dream of winning a race in a rowboat of any kind will be successful in their dealings with the opposite sex.

To be defeated augurs the loss of your sweetheart through a rival.

**RUBY.** Dreaming of a ruby is a forerunner of success in business or in the winning of the person you love.

If a woman dreams of losing one, her lover will be indifferent.

**RUINS.** To dream of ruins portends that lovers will break their engagement. This is particularly true if the ruins are seen by moonlight.

## S

**SAFE.** To dream of owning a safe portends that you will overcome discouraging conditions relative to a love affair.

**SAGE.** If a maiden dreams of using this savory herb to give flavor to food, it is a sign that she guard against allowing her sweetheart to make extravagant expenditures for her.

**SAILOR.** Dreaming of a sailor—including both those of the navy and the merchant marine of any country—is a prediction that the dreamer, if a woman, will lose her love through a tendency to flirt with other men.

If a man dreams that he is a sailor, he should beware of designing women.

**SALAD.** If a young woman dreams of making salad, it signifies that her sweetheart will be temperamental and that she will be subject to his moods.

**SALMON.** To dream of salmon leaping up a swift stream, is a sign to a young unmarried woman that her future husband will be happy-go-lucky, and as fortunate in business matters as he is in social affairs.

**SALT.** If a maiden dreams of eating salt, she will find that through her lack of enthusiasm she will unconsciously turn her sweetheart away from her. His growing interest in another girl will show her that she has made a mistake.

**SAPPHIRE.** This is a gem that indicates to a woman that her lover will be dependable in all important matters.

**SARDINES.** To dream of serving sardines to a group of guests is a sign to a young woman that she will be loved by someone from a lower station in life whose affections she cannot return.

**SASH.** A dream of wearing a sash predicts that you will have to make excuses for the behavior of your lover.

If a young woman buys a sash in a dream, she will secure the lasting admiration of her sweetheart by her cleverness and efficiency.

**SATAN.** A woman who dreams of seeing Satan should be warned against unseemly behavior with the opposite sex. It is a sign that one's present sweetheart will prove to be unworthy of trust.

**SCALES** (*See also* Weighing). It is fortunate for a young woman to dream of weighing her lover, and the heavier he seems to be in the dream the greater are the indications that he will be a man of solid worth, both in his personality and income.

SCANDAL. One is not likely to marry within a long time after dreaming of a scandal.

SCISSORS. Dreams of scissors are unlucky. They are portentous of quarrels between lovers or between husbands and wives.

SCULPTOR. An augury of honors or pursuit from men of wealth and position is contained in a woman's dream that her sweetheart is a sculptor.

SEA (See Ocean). A maiden who dreams of being on a calm, blue sea with her sweetheart has every reason for expecting a happy outcome to her love affair.

SEDUCERS. A man who dreams of seduction should be on his guard against false accusers.
    If his sweetheart is affronted by proposals that he may make, he will be assured that the woman he loves is above reproach.

SHAKING HANDS (See Hands). If you dream of shaking hands with persons whose social station is beneath yours, it is an indication that your lover will honor you for your kindness and straightforwardness.

SHAKESPEARE. To dream of reading Shakespeare or of seeing him in person, is an indication that your love affair will be straightforward and sincere.

SHAVING (See Beard). A man who dreams of shaving may expect to solve any problems which may have arisen in connection with his love affair.
    A woman who dreams of shaving should look to her conduct in the company of the opposite sex.

SHAWL. If a young woman dreams of losing a shawl, it is a sign that she may be jilted by her sweetheart.

SHIP. To dream of a shipwreck is indicative of betrayal by familiar acquaintances.

**SHIRT.** A person who dreams of putting on his or her shirt will very likely be estranged from his sweetheart.

Losing one's shirt is a forerunner of disgrace in business or love.

**SHOEMAKER.** It is a sign that a woman will have no financial troubles if she dreams that her husband or sweetheart is a shoemaker.

**SHOES.** Divorce is predicted if a person dreams of losing his or her shoes.

To lose one shoe is a sign of quarrels.

**SILK.** A young woman who dreams of old silk dresses will be sought in marriage by a rich old man.

Silk which is soiled or worn out indicates that, unless she is careful, she will disgrace her family.

**SINGER** (*See* Actor). The portent of hearing someone sing in a dream is auspicious when the selection is melodious and in tune. To those who are in love it augurs a successful culmination of their affair.

A singer whose song is off key, or otherwise disagreeable, indicates quarrels with one's lover.

**SKIDDING** (*See* Motor Car). To dream that you are driving an automobile on a slippery pavement and it skids, is a sign that one should exercise extreme caution not to do anything which may impair the confidence of one's sweetheart.

**SLAUGHTERHOUSE.** Your lover will fear you if you dream of watching the operations in a slaughterhouse. This is a warning to those who are inclined to be overbearing.

**SLEEP.** If a young man or a young woman dreams of sleeping with his or her lover, it is a sign that either should exercise great caution in the development of their affair.

142

A dream of sleeping with someone who is repulsive augurs ill in matters of the heart.

To sleep beside a small child predicts that your love will be reciprocated by your sweetheart.

Sleeping alone in a bed with clean, fresh linen is a favorable sign to those in love.

SLEIGH. Failure in a love affair is foretold by dreaming of either seeing or riding in a sleigh.

If the sleigh is overturned, you may regard it as a fortunate augury, for it will be a warning against some ill-advised move on your part.

SLIDING. It is a sign that your sweetheart will fail to keep his or her promises if you dream of sliding.

SLIP (*See* Petticoat). To dream of seeing a handsome brunette wearing a slip, foretells good fortune in both love and financial affairs.

If the wearer of the slip is a blonde, or red headed, it is a warning against plots which may work harm to your plans for matrimony.

SLIPPERS. Scandalous doings are foretold by a dream of slippers, and, therefore, this dream should be regarded as a warning against intrigue. Even mild flirtations should be avoided after such a dream.

SMELLING. The odor of fresh flowers smelled in a dream predicts happy days of courtship.

The smell of burning wood or of autumn leaves is a forerunner of an early marriage and pleasant home ties.

Perfumes are a harbinger of intrigue.

Disagreeable odors of any kind indicate broken engagements.

SNAKE (*See* Asp). A maiden who dreams of her lover handling a poisonous snake will have reason to admire his bravery, but if she dreams that he is bitten by the snake, it is an augury of misfortune.

**SNOW.** True love will be requited if you dream of seeing a snowstorm from inside of a warm house.

If the flakes are large, your mate will be a wealthy and generous person.

If the flakes are small and powdery, it is a sign of a struggle of some kind before you will achieve happiness.

**SOCKS** (*See* Stockings). To dream of putting on socks foretells, for a maiden, an indiscreet situation that will arise with her lover. For a man it is a warning against unfaithfulness.

If a woman dreams of attending church wearing short socks, it is a forerunner of quarrels with her husband or sweetheart.

Washing socks in a dream is an augury of both a successful love affair and a happy married life.

**SOLES** (*See* Heels). It is bad luck to dream that there is a hole in the sole of your shoe. It portends a broken engagement.

Rubber soles are a sign of happiness in love.

**SOOT.** Quarrels with lover, husband, wife or friend are portended by a dream of soot.

**SOUP** (*See* Broth). To dream of seeing anyone eating soup is an indication to unmarried folk that they will have many opportunities to make a favorable match.

A woman who dreams of making soup has much to look forward to, for she will be loved well by her husband.

**SPARROWS.** If one dreams of feeding sparrows, it is a sign that the dreamer will be adored by a person of the opposite sex and will lead a life of elegant ease.

**SPEED BOAT.** A whirlwind courtship and marriage will come to the man or maid who dreams of driving a speed boat.

144

SPIDER. Family or lovers' quarrels are foretold by a dream of killing a spider.

To destroy a spider's web is a sign that someone will make cruel accusations against your honor.

SQUINTING. If a young person dreams that his or her lover is continually squinting, he or she will be caught in a compromising situation.

STAGE (See Play, Actor, Dancing, Singer). A dream of a stage set for the rising of the curtain predicts that you will have an experience of unusual importance to your sweetheart and one which will require you to make a lengthy explanation.

If there is any action at all upon the stage, the dream must be interpreted by referring to one of the headings indicated above.

STAIRS. For a person of either sex to dream of walking down stairs is an indication that he or she should be prepared for an unhappy climax to what seemed to be a love affair of great moment.

STATUES. If a statue of marble is seen in a dream, there will be a prolonged period of indifference on the part of your beloved.

STETHOSCOPE. A dream of seeing someone being tested with a stethoscope, indicates that there will be recurring disputes and frequent reconciliations between you and your lover.

STOCKINGS (See Socks). To dream of silk stockings bodes no good to either man or maid. It is an indication of coming pleasures through dissolute companionship with members of the opposite sex.

If a woman finds a hole in her stocking she should think twice before throwing herself too heartily into a love affair that may leave an unforgettable impression upon her.

Cotton stockings seen in a dream are a forerunner

of some untoward event that will seem to prove the reality of life.

Net stockings are a precursor of the revelation of some secret that you would wish to keep hidden.

Wool stockings presage a message from someone of the opposite sex who wishes you well.

Half-length stockings (*see* Socks).

**STRAWBERRIES.** Eating strawberries in a dream is a good sign to lovers. It indicates a happy culmination to one's affair if the berries are sweet and of good flavor. If the strawberries appear to be unripe or sour, it is a prediction of quarrels that may be pleasantly adjusted.

**STRUMPET** (*See* Prostitute, Harlot).

**SWAMP.** Love affairs will be tangled if you dream of walking precariously through swampy land.

**SWEARING** (*See also* Profanity). If a person in love dreams of hearing his or her sweetheart swearing, it is an almost sure indication that there is unfaithfulness.

A maiden who has this dream should look to her own conduct, especially if the profanity she hears is understandable to her.

**SWEETHEART.** It is an unfortunate augury if you dream that your sweetheart is dead. You may expect ill luck in your married life.

To dream of your sweetheart being delightful to your sight and senses is an augury of a happy married life, with children who will be a credit to you.

**SWIMMING.** A maiden who dreams that she is swimming with someone, either man or woman, who is a much better swimmer, may look forward to a life of ease and many exciting love affairs.

# T

**TACKS.** A woman who dreams of driving tacks will be sure

of overcoming any rival who seeks to outdo her with regard to a man's affections.

TALISMAN. If a maiden dreams that her lover gives her a talisman of any kind, it is a sign that her fondest wishes with regard to romance will be fulfilled.

TAPESTRY. A dream of tapestry in one's rooms is a prediction of a marriage that will be financially advantageous to the dreamer.

TEA. Love difficulties are foretold by a dream of seeing dregs in the bottom of your tea.

TEASING. Either teasing a person or being teased in a dream is a portent of success in all matters pertaining to the grand passion.

TELEPHONE. Rivals in love are predicted by a dream of talking over the telephone.
    Having difficulty in understanding what is said over the telephone is an augury of lovers' quarrels and a possible broken engagement.

THEATRE (*See* Stage).

THIGH. A maiden who dreams of admiring her own thigh is likely to become involved in an exciting and dangerous adventure with a man.
    To admire another's thigh indicates that one will choose a sweetheart for his or her sterling character.

TOBACCO. To dream of seeing men smoking predicts the solution of a problem pertaining to someone you love.
    Women smoking cigarettes are an augury of contentment in the home.
    Women smoking pipes foretell quarrels and disappointments.

TOOTHBRUSH. If you dream that you are brushing your teeth and the bristles come out in your mouth, it is a good sign. To a maiden it foretells success in a love affair, followed by a happy marriage and a large family.

**TOPAZ.** To dream of being presented with a piece of jewelry containing a topaz is an indication that someone loves you more than he or she is able to express in words.

**TORTURE.** If you dream of seeing someone being tortured, and endeavor to help the person, it is a sign that you will be successful only after a long struggle to hold your sweetheart.

**TRAFFIC SIGNALS.** *Green* shows that you should proceed cautiously with any. investment that you may be contemplating, or with any love affair that may have started.

*Yellow* indicates that you should ask for the best possible advice on your affairs, and follow it.

*Red* is a good portent provided a halt of some kind is made; otherwise it is a prediction that someone in whom you believe will prove untrue.

**TRIANGLE.** The end of a love affair is predicted by a dream of a triangle of any kind.

**TRIPLETS** (*See* Twins, Quadruplets, Quintuplets). Disappointment in love, but success in wealth is presaged to a maiden who dreams that she has triplets.

**TRUNK.** A maiden who dreams of unsuccessfully trying to open a trunk will be wooed by a wealthy man, but through misunderstanding will fail to marry him.

**TUNNEL.** Difficulties in love are presaged by a dream of walking through a tunnel, or going through one in a train.

**TURNIPS.** A young woman who dreams of planting turnip seed will almost certainly win a good looking and wealthy husband.

**TURQUOISE.** Great irritations in a love affair will come to a person who dreams of having a turquoise ring, or other piece of jewelry, stolen.

A woman who dreams of stealing a turquoise will suffer for a too hasty love affair.

**TWINS** (*See* Triplets, Quadruplets, Quintuplets). To dream of having twins, foretells to a woman that she will be surprised by hearing from a former lover who lives at a great distance.

## U

**UGLINESS.** Dreaming of a person with an ugly face bodes no good to young lovers.

A maiden who dreams that she is ugly either in face or in disposition will have a quarrel with her sweetheart.

**UMBRELLA.** Walking in the rain with a leaky umbrella is a dream which portends a strained situation between you and your sweetheart.

**UNIFORM.** For a maiden to dream of wearing a man's uniform, either military or naval, is a sign that she will be involved in a scandal with a man who is less to blame than she is.

If she dreams of removing the uniform in a public place she should regard it as a warning against indulging her love for adventurous escapades.

## V

**VACCINATION.** A man dreaming of being vaccinated is likely to be unduly influenced by feminine charmers.

**VALENTINE.** It is a sign that you will lose opportunities of making a suitable match if you dream of sending valentines.

A maiden who receives a valentine is likely to marry beneath her in spite of the advice of her parents.

**VALLEY.** Happy courtship days are predicted by a dream of finding oneself walking through a verdant valley.

**VASE.** A dream of breaking a cloisonné vase is a portent of a happy solution of problems relating to persons of the opposite sex.

Kicking a vase that is on the floor is an augury of discovering the perfidy of a lover.

To drink from a vase is a warning against a love affair which your better judgment would consider inappropriate.

**VEGETABLES.** A maiden who dreams that she is preparing vegetables in the kitchen will be likely to lose a lover through a stand-offish attitude that will prove too much for him to combat.

**VEIL.** A woman who wears a veil in a dream must guard against insincerity with her lover.

If she dreams that she loses a veil, it is an indication that her lover will find out that she is deceitful.

**VELVET.** To dream that she is wearing a velvet gown predicts to a young woman that she will receive attentions from several wealthy men.

**VERANDA.** To dream that one is seated with a lover on a veranda, is to be able to look forward to happiness through an early marriage or through home delights.

**VICAR.** A woman who dreams of marrying a vicar is in danger of failing to secure the affection of a man whom she admires.

If she dreams that she is wooed by a vicar, it is a sign that she will either not marry at all, or that she will marry unwisely to avoid being a spinster.

**VICTORY.** The winning of a victory in a dream is a

prediction of success in resisting temptation and in all love affairs.

VINEYARD. It is good luck to dream of a vineyard, for it is a prediction of successful lovemaking.

VIOLETS. A young woman who dreams of picking violets will soon meet the man whom she will marry.

Violets that are withered, or that one finds pressed between the leaves of books, denote disappointment in matters pertaining to the heart.

VOW. To dream that you make a vow, indicates a happy culmination of a love affair.

If you listen to someone else making a vow in a dream, it is a sign of your having to go through troublous times in connection with an engagement.

VOYAGE. Ill luck in love affairs is foretold by dreaming of disaster on a sea voyage.

# W

WAFER. A maiden who dreams of baking wafers will be likely to worry considerably about remaining a spinster.

If she dreams of eating wafers, it is a sign that she is over particular in her choice of men friends.

WAGON. (*See* Motor Car). If one dreams of riding in a wagon drawn by a horse, or team of horses, it is an augury of an unhappy married life.

If the wagon is drawn by a mule, or a team of these animals, it foretells marriage with a person who is hard to get along with.

WAIST. A woman who dreams that her waist is torn will find that she is open to criticism for misbehavior of one kind of another.

To try on a waist, indicates that she will have rivals for the affection of her sweetheart; but if she has no difficulty adjusting the garment, this rivalry will have no ill effect.

WAKE. It portends misfortune for a young woman to dream of seeing her lover at a wake, for it means that she will make some careless move which will make people think less of her.

WALNUT. A maiden who dreams that her hands are stained with walnut is likely to lose her lover to another young woman.

WALTZ (*See* Dancing). To move in a smooth and pleasant waltz with the object of your affections, is a forerunner of great happiness in the married state.

WAR. It is a forerunner of news detrimental to her lover's reputation if a maiden dreams of his going to war.

WASHBOWL. If you dream of bathing your face and hands in a washbowl, it is a prediction of an early perfect understanding with the object of your affections.

WASHERWOMAN. It bodes no good for a woman to dream that she washes clothes for a living, for it is a sign that she will be careless of her reputation in her dealings with men.

WASHING. If you dream of washing yourself, it is an indication that you will be thought well of by most members of the opposite sex, and may look forward to a happy married life.

WATER. A maiden may look forward to a sudden awakening to love if she dreams of playing in the water.
    A dream of having water sprayed on the head, or being rained on, is a sign of a coming violent love affair.

WEDDING (*See also* Bride, Marriage). A young woman who dreams of having a secret wedding is in danger of extremely bad luck in connection with her love affairs.

If she dreams of marriage in church in the approved manner, it is a portent of a happy married life.

If parental objections are indicated in a dream, it is probable that she will be criticized for her actions.

Dreaming that her lover marries another girl is an augury of an early marriage with little to worry about.

Anyone who dreams of being married should be warned of an approaching death. This augury may be considerably mitigated if the wedding appears to be attended by a great many happy people.

To dream of a wedding guest dressed in black is a portent of unhappiness in marriage.

**WEDDING RING.** A man who dreams of wearing a wedding ring will be likely to find that his wife is intolerant of his careless habits.

If a woman dreams that her wedding ring is bright and untarnished, it is a sign that she will be happy in her married life.

**WEDGE.** Lovers who dream of a wedge, or wedge-shaped article, are likely to be separated from the object of their affections.

**WEDLOCK.** To dream that one is unhappy in his or her married life, foretells an affair which will cause great difficulty. There is every reason to look forward to a family scandal or unusual situations from which it will be difficult to be released.

It is fortunate for a woman to dream that she is happily married to a man of wealth and good breeding.

**WEEPING.** A young woman who dreams of weeping will have a quarrel with her lover, probably through her own unreasonable attitude.

**WEEVIL.** False love is indicated by a dream of weevils.

**WEIGHING** (*See* Scales). If a maiden dreams that she is being weighed on the same scales with her lover, it is a sign that he will always comply with her wishes.

**WETNESS.** A woman who dreams that she is wet from rain or any other cause is likely to be implicated in some disgraceful affair.

**WHEAT.** It is a fortunate augury to see wheat in storage, for it means that your love affairs will proceed smoothly toward a happy culmination.

**WHIRLWIND.** A young woman who dreams that she is in the center of a whirlwind which blows her skirts upward is very likely to get into scandalous difficulties through secret flirtations.

**WHITEWASH.** A dream of whitewash portends estrangement between lovers and the probability of being deceived by someone who has been trusted.

**WIDOW.** There is disappointment in store for a man who dreams that he marries a widow. Some undertaking which means a great deal to him will fail.

**WIFE.** If a wife dreams that her husband pets her, it is a sign of unusually upset conditions in the home.

A man who dreams that his wife is more than ordinarily affable is likely to profit largely from an important commercial undertaking.

**WIND** (*See* Zephyr). Wind soughing through the trees portrays estrangement from the person you love the best. If you dream of being buffeted by the wind, it is a sign of disappointment in love.

**WINDOW.** A dream of a broken window is a forerunner of disloyalty from someone you love.

**WINE.** A maiden who dreams of drinking wine will marry a man of wealth, position and taste.

**WOODEN SHOE** (*See also* Shoes). This is a dream which is a forerunner of a destructive element entering your life through your love affairs.

WOODPILE. Misunderstandings in love are betokened by dreaming of a woodpile.

To dream of working at a woodpile, either sawing or piling logs, is a sign of failure to make marriage a success.

## Y

YARN. A young woman who dreams of winding yarn may regard it as a preliminary to an early love affair with a man who will be worthy of her affection.

YEARNING. If a maiden dreams of a man's yearning for her, she will have an early proposal from someone whom she admires.

YEW TREE. A girl who dreams of sitting under a yew tree will have many worries concerning the faithfulness of her lover.

If she sees her lover standing beside a yew tree, it is probable that she will hear that he is ill or in danger.

## Z

ZENITH. To dream of lying on the ground and gazing straight up to the zenith, is a prediction of great happiness with the man or woman of your choice.

ZEPHYR (See Wind). To dream of listening to the soft sounds of zephyrs, is a portent of deceit by a lover.

# GOOD LUCK DREAMS

## CHAPTER V

Under this heading are listed the dreams that prophesy advantageous happenings and conditions; that predict the receipt of money—through gift, inheritance, investment, or as a result of labors; that assure honors, happiness, contentment and so on. There are no love dreams here. They are interpreted in their own chapter, both for better and worse.

It should be remembered that the conditions of a dream determine its prophecy. Clouds are listed in this chapter, but in another part of the book, under different conditions, they are given as a portent of distinctly bad luck. Under *Cleanliness,* interpreted herein, it is a fortunate sign if you dream of washing your own clothes, while elsewhere it points out that misfortune is predicted if you dream of washing someone else's garments.

This is a good place to repeat that the way to get the nearly complete interpretation of your dream is to look up the subject in the index at the back of the book, and refer to all the pages listed under it. Then look up the major features of the dream in the same way, so that you will know of other influences that may have a bearing on the outcome.

May you have many of the dreams listed in this chapter!

### GOOD LUCK DREAMS

### A

ABANDONMENT. A man who dreams of abandoning a mistress will inherit money from a hitherto unexpected source.

157

**ABBEY.** To dream that a priest prevents your entering an abbey is a prediction that your enemies will be powerless to effect your ruin.

**ABBESS.** It is a presage of excellent prospects in all ways to dream that an abbess smiles upon you.

**ABDOMEN.** If you have a pain in your abdomen in a dream, it is a forerunner of good health and prosperity.

**ABDUCTION.** You will be successful in your plans if you dream of being carried off by force.

**ABROAD.** To dream of going abroad, or going to a foreign country foretells a trip in the company of pleasant people, with fortunate results.

**ABSENCE.** Rejoicing over the absence of an acquaintance in a dream is a prediction that you will not have any further cause to worry about the activity of an enemy.

**ABUNDANCE.** Whatever may be abundant—love, money, friends—such a dream is a sign of success in the plans nearest your heart.

**ABUSE.** It is a good sign to dream that you are abusing someone else. It presages success through your own efforts.

**ABYSS.** Looking into an abyss, but escaping from falling into it, is a portent of the successful solution of a difficult problem.

**ACCEPTANCE.** For a man to dream that one of his business propositions has been accepted is an indication that he is on the road to financial success.

**ACCORDION.** Hearing the music of this instrument is a presage of cheering news that will make your daily burdens lighter.

**ACORNS.** Lucky is he or she who dreams of acorns, either on the tree or on the ground. They are a portent of success in an undertaking that is close to your heart.

Picking them from a tree indicates that you will successfully solve a harassing problem.

**ACQUITTAL.** An inheritance of considerable value is foretold by a dream of being acquitted of a crime or misdemeanor.

**ACTOR OR ACTRESS.** A handsome actor or a beautiful actress seen in a dream predicts immediate comfort and freedom from worry.

**ADDING MACHINE.** If you dream of using an adding machine, you will meet someone who will prove his or her friendship by substantial co-operation.

**ADIEUS** (*See* Forsaking). Pleasant adieus to friends are a presage of delightful social activity.

**ADMIRATION.** A dream that you have the admiration of the public or friends is a sign that persistent attention to your work will bring hoped-for rewards.

**ADOPTED.** An adopted son, seen in a dream, portends success in speculation.

**ADULTERY.** This dream is propitious only when it is of a temptation overcome.

**ADVANCEMENT.** Business or social advancement is a dream that may be expected to come true, although the need for a continued effort will always be present.

**ADVERSARY** (*See* Enemy).

**ADVICE.** To dream of being sensibly advised by an older or wiser person than yourself is a sign that the future holds rich rewards for you in money, honor and friendship.

AFFLUENCE (*See* Wealth).

AGATE. An agate, either in a ring or in other pieces of jewelry, or unmounted, presages a moderate increase in income.

ALBUM. Looking at a photograph album in a dream is a harbinger of some small triumph that will give you great pleasure.

ALMONDS. Eating salted almonds is a lucky sign if they are wholesome and of good flavor. This dream foretells a sudden acquisition of wealth.

ALUMINUM. Shiny aluminum pots, pans or other utensils are harbingers of that greatest blessing—contentment.

AMATEUR. A dream of a person who pursues an art or a craft because he or she loves it instead of as a means of making money (which is the real meaning of "Amateur") is a sign that your expectations of life will be fulfilled.

AMETHYST. Contentment with a modest but adequate income is the prophecy contained in a dream about an amethyst.

AMMUNITION. This dream portends the beginning of an important undertaking and its successful termination.

ANCHOR. It is good luck to dream of seeing an anchor out of water, for it predicts news of financial success.

ANDIRONS. Good will between you and your acquaintance is predicted by a dream of andirons on which there is burning wood.

ANECDOTES. If you are telling anecdotes to children in a dream, it is a sign that people of high station in life will like you. It also foretells that you will develop qualities that will make you successful in the long run.

**ANGELS.** A pleasant dream in which angels figure is a forerunner of a legacy from someone you do not know.

**ANGLING.** To dream of fishing is a good augury; better if you catch anything.

**ANVIL.** To see a workman hammering hot iron on an anvil is a sign of success in the work you are doing. If hot sparks fly at each stroke, the dream is particularly favorable.

**APPAREL.** A yellow dress seen in a dream means that you will have happiness and make money.

   To dream that you are wearing new clothes that are fashionable and of good fit is an augury of good fortune.

**APPLES.** A dream of seeing red apples growing on a tree whose foliage is green predicts good news from an unexpected source.

**APRIL.** Reference in a dream to the month of April is a propitious sign. A dream of April sunshine predicts the successful completion of an important work.

**ARCH.** To pass through a large stone arch means that your efforts to achieve distinction and wealth will be rewarded.

**ARCHBISHOP.** A young woman who dreams of this dignitary will make friends who will be of great use to her.

**ARMHOLE.** Success in your business, trade or profession is predicted if you dream of tearing the armhole of your coat.

**AROMA.** A girl will receive a valuable gift if she dreams of smelling a pleasing aroma.

**ARROWS.** An end to suffering and the beginning of a round of gayety are to be expected by those who dream of arrows.

**ASPARAGUS.** Dreaming of this vegetable in any way is the prelude to prosperity. Eating it portends continued success.

**ASYLUM.** To dream that you have been committed to an insane asylum is an excellent omen. It is a prophecy that your mental powers will increase, and that you will be looked up to for your good judgment.

**AUCTION.** Success in business dealings follows a dream of attending an auction. To buy an article at such a sale indicates a new and advantageous business association.

**AUTHOR.** If an author dreams that his or her manuscript has been rejected by a publisher, it is a sign that an acceptance will follow before long.

# B

**BABY.** A baby just beginning to walk without assistance is a dream that presages a spirit of independence and, through this, great success.

To dream of seeing a baby in a baby carriage means that you will have many good times in the company of a friend. Twin babies in a carriage denote wealth.

**BACKBONE.** Seen in a dream, a backbone is a sign of contentment.

**BACON.** Eating bacon is a portent of general good luck.

**BADGER.** You will overcome adverse conditions in business if you dream of this animal.

**BAKER OR BAKING.** To see someone baking in a dream means that a pressing problem will be solved in a satisfactory manner.

**BALDHEAD.** A baldheaded baby is a prediction of a happy home life.

162

**BANANAS.** A large, well-ripened bunch of bananas seen in a dream, augurs well for the dreamer.

**BANDY LEGS.** To dream of having bandy legs is a prediction of an improvement in your business affairs.

**BANISHMENT.** If you dream that you are banished from home or country, you will enjoy a long season of prosperity.

**BANQUET.** The prediction of dreaming that you are a guest at a sumptuous banquet is that you will be selected by someone of authority to hold a position of profit and trust.

**BARROOM.** Staunch loyalty from your family and friends is foretold by dreaming of being in a barroom.

To see women drinking at a bar is a prediction of lighthearted gayety.

**BASEBALL.** Contentment is the forecast of a baseball game attended in a dream.

**BASIN.** A girl who dreams of bathing or washing her hands or feet in a basin will make many good friends of both sexes.

**BATHING** (*See* Cleanliness). If one dreams of taking a bath in clean water with good results, he or she may expect an improvement in both material and spiritual conditions.

**BATTLE** (*See* Fight).

**BEADS.** To dream that you are counting beads of any kind means great good luck; if you are stringing them, it is a sign of riches.

**BEATING.** Marital happiness is foretold by a man's

dreaming that he is beating his wife. Fathers or mothers who dream of beating their children will be blessed with more offspring.

BEAUTY. Good business is predicted by a dream of beauty. To dream of a beautiful woman is a forerunner of luck in a business deal.

BEAVERS. These animals foretell of material success through hard luck.

BED. If one dreams of sleeping on a bed out-of-doors, it is a sign that he or she will have a pleasant and profitable experience.

BEES. Bees are a lucky dream if one is not stung by them. They are an augury of pleasant occupations, and of new and profitable responsibilities.

BEETS. Good news is prophesied by a dream of eating beets or seeing them growing.
    A dream of putting beets on to boil is a sign that you will solve a problem that has proved distressing.

BEQUEST. To dream of making a bequest, either of money or articles of value, predicts that you will be surprised by the receipt of money that is totally unexpected.

BICYCLE. Prospects of uncommon brightness are foretold by a dream of riding a bicycle uphill if you do not dismount before reaching the top.

BIRDS. Prosperity is predicted if you dream of seeing birds of any kind on the wing.

BLANKETS. Clean fluffy blankets are a presage of good fortune in all directions.

BLOSSOMS. To dream of seeing blossoms on trees or bushes is a sign that you will be greatly pleased by some business development or good news.

**BOOKS.** Studying books in a dream is a portent of honors to be conferred on you.

If you see children reading books, it foretells harmony in your family and among your friends.

**BOOTS.** Luck in business is foretold by a dream of wearing new boots.

**BOUQUET.** A lovely bouquet of fresh flowers predicts that you will inherit a considerable sum of money.

**BOW AND ARROW.** Through someone's misfortune you will amass great wealth if you have this dream.

**BOX.** It is splendid fortune to open a box in a dream. Wealth, with all it can bring in comforts and freedom from worry will be yours.

**BRACELET.** Material gains will come to those who dream of finding a bracelet.

**BRAINS.** To eat brains in a dream augurs an increase in knowledge and the power to think with profitable effect.

**BRASS.** Dreams of brass articles foretell an improvement in your job or your family life.

**BREAD.** If one dreams of baking bread, it is a sign that your financial worries are over.

**BREATH.** In a dream, if you mark the sweetness of another person's breath, it is an omen of a long life and success in business.

**BRONCHITIS.** If you dream of having this disease, it is a sign that with suitable training and study you will achieve great distinction as a singer.

**BRUSHING.** Using a brush to remove dust from your

clothing or shoes foretells just payment for arduous labors.

BUGLE. Hearing a clear, sweet bugle call is a portent of good news from some quarter where it is least expected.

BUILDINGS. Magnificent edifices in excellent condition, with well kept grounds, are an augury that you will rise to the top of the profession or business in which you are engaged.

BULLDOG. To dream of having a friendly bulldog is a forerunner of good fortune and of financial assistance when you need it.

BURNS. Good news is predicted by a dream of being burned.

BUTTER. Eating or selling fresh butter foretells an improvement in your social and financial condition.

BUTTERFLY. A single butterfly seen fluttering in a field or garden is a prediction of contentment through freedom from worry.

BUTTONS. A successful career is promised to a young man who dreams of seeing bright buttons on a uniform.

## C

CAB. It is an augury of having fun to dream of riding in a cab, either horse-drawn or motor-propelled. This fun may come from association with bright, clever people, from attending parties, or from indulging in hobbies such as photography, stamp collecting, or outdoor sports.

CADDY. To dream of playing golf and having a caddy foretells that you will receive a present that you expected.

CALMNESS. This is a fortunate dream, as it is a prediction of a calm, well-ordered life.

**CAMEL.** If you dream of owning a camel, it is a sign that a mining investment will turn out well.

**CAMP.** Domestic peace is foretold by a dream of being in a camp of many people, either military or civilian.

**CAN.** To dream of opening a can indicates a pleasant surprise.
Drinking out of a can presages profit on any business deal in which you are engaged.
Throwing away an empty can means that you will solve a problem that has been very distressing.

**CANDY.** Eating candy in a dream is prophetic of a smooth-running household without serious worries.

**CAP.** An inheritance is foretold to one who dreams of seeing a miner wearing a cap.

**CAPTAIN.** Any aspirations to higher things which you may have had will be likely to come true if you dream of a captain, whether in the military service or of a less important branch.

**CARROTS.** General good luck and financial prosperity are portended by a dream of eating or seeing carrots growing. It is likewise fortunate to dream of preparing them for cooking.

**CASK.** If you dream of seeing a cask filled with good things, either to eat or drink, it augurs well for your future ability to pay up all your debts.

**CASTLE.** To dream of owning or living in a castle foreshadows a luxurious life in which your resources will enable you to live according to your personal desires or whims.

**CATTLE.** You may expect a prosperous and interesting

future if you dream of well-conditioned cattle grazing in pleasant pastures.

CAULIFLOWER. Good health is predicted by a dream of this succulent vegetable. Seeing it growing predicts an improvement in your financial affairs.

CAVALRY. To see a group of cavalrymen in a dream is a forerunner of an improvement in your business, or social standing, or both.

CEDARS. Green, well-formed cedar trees seen in a dream are significant to those who are engaged in a new undertaking, and presage a successful enterprise.

CELERY. Like most fresh vegetables, celery augurs well for the person who dreams about it. The prediction is of general good fortune.

CELLAR. A well-stocked cellar, whether with food, wine, or coal is a presage of contentment.

CEMETERY. If the cemetery of which you dream is well kept, it is a sign that you will overcome all the obstacles that confront you.

CHAIRMAN. A dream of being chairman of any kind of meeting points toward a popularity that you will win through kindness and consideration for others.

CHAMBER. To dream of finding yourself in a bedchamber of luxurious appointments, your immediate future will hold a sudden and unexpected increase in fortune.

CHAMPION. A new and warm friendship is foretold by dreaming of a champion in any line of sport.

CHAPEL. If you dream of being outside a chapel, you will be surprised by sudden good fortune.

CHASTISE. It is lucky to dream of chastising your children

168

if in the dream you believe it is justified.

**CHECKS.** Good luck in money matters will follow a dream of receiving checks.

**CHEEKS.** Dreaming of your own cheeks, especially if they seem to be without blemish, points toward a happy outcome of a disagreement.

**CHERRIES.** Eating red cherries in a dream is a portent of getting the thing you want most at the moment.
White cherries predict the making of new and lasting friendships.

**CHILDREN.** A dream of lovely children could foretell only great blessings and a happy home.
For a married woman to dream of giving birth to a child is an augury of domestic bliss and freedom from worry.

**CHIMES.** Chimes heard in a dream are an omen of joy through understanding of one's mate, family or friends.

**CHIMNEYS.** Something good will happen to you if you dream of chimneys, whether short or tall. Smoke pouring from chimneys is an especially good sign.

**CHINA.** Money is in sight for you if you dream of china dishes, but you may have to wait some time for it as it is coming from a considerable distance.

**CHOCOLATE.** To drink chocolate in a dream is a sign of good health.
Eating sweet chocolate denotes that someone will do you a great favor. Eating chocolate candies portends comfort in old age.

**CHOKING.** Good luck may be expected if you dream of choking, although it will come after some struggle.

**CHRISTMAS.** Any dream pertaining to this holiday is of

fortunate augury. It foretells happiness with one's family and one's friends.

CHURCH. To see a church from a distance predicts a happy solution of a problem that has oppressed you.

CHURN. One who dreams of churning may rest assured that their troubles will cease to bother them.

CIGAR. For a man to dream of smoking a cigar is a sign that he will be prosperous through his own efforts.

CIGARETTE. To dream of lighting one cigarette from another, either your own or someone else's, portends an improvement in your financial affiars.

CLEANLINESS. Where this quality is indicated in any form except where cleaning is done for hire, it is an omen of an improvement in existing conditions.
Cleaning house portends a welcome visitor.
Cleaning or polishing silverware or jewelry augurs the receipt of money.
To dream of bathing is a sign that you will have the respect of all with whom you come in contact.
To dream of washing your own undergarments indicates that you will preserve your self-respect through all situations.

CLIMBING. If you reach the goal of your climb in a dream, you will overcome a difficulty that may have been troubling you.

CLOCK. A clock dream is a good omen if you hear it strike the hour.

CLOTHES. To wear smart clothes in a dream presages popularity in both the business and social worlds.

CLOUDS. If they are colored with the glow of the setting sun, clouds are a portent of an easy life.

**CLOVER.** Blossoming clover in a field or lawn predicts that your higher ambitions will be realized in full.

If you pick clover blossoms, the prediction is that peace of mind will be added to your other good fortunes.

**CLUB.** To be threatened or struck by a person with a club is a sign that you will get the better of those who seek to defame your character.

**COAL.** A brightly glowing coal fire predicts cheerful surroundings and the company of friends you love.

**COAT.** Wearing an old coat or a ragged coat denotes success in some literary venture.

**COAT-OF-ARMS.** This is a good omen for those who need protection against evil forces. If it is in color, look up the significance of that which predominates.

**COCKCROW.** Good news may be expected by one who dreams of hearing a cock crow.

**COINS.** Dreams about coins are most lucky if the coins are copper. Next in order are gold coins, with silver last.

**COLORS.** It is good luck to dream of many bright colors. The significance of each of the colors, arranged in the order of their luckiness, is as follows:

*Red:* a long and vigorous life.
*Blue:* peaceful and harmonious family relationships.
*Green:* ability to make money.
*White:* distinction in the community in which you live.
*Orange:* you will own your own home.
*Purple:* sufficient money for your needs.
*Yellow:* jealousy will be shown toward you.
*Brown:* accusations of dishonesty.
*Black:* bad luck generally.

The shades and variations of colors have a bearing on their significance; the brighter they are, the more propitious.

**COLLECTION.** To give a contribution when a collection is being made predicts that you will take a trip that will have profitable and interesting results.

**COLT.** A dream of a colt frisking in a green pasture is an omen of a period of happy relaxation.

**COLUMBINE.** This flower seen in a dream is a portent of a trip to an unusual and delightful place.

**COLUMNIST.** To dream of a man or woman who writes a daily newspaper column is to be assured that through arduous labor you will acquire a competency.

**COMEDY** (*See* Actor). The quality of comedy, humor, or fun in a dream usually means that you will acquire a goodly sum of money.

**COMIC SONGS.** It is a lucky sign to dream of hearing someone sing comic songs.

**COMPANIONS.** To dream that you are in the company of one or more pleasant companions is an augury of fortunate investments.

**COMPASS.** Prosperity is foretold by a dream of looking at the needle of a mariner's compass aboard ship.

**COMPLETION.** A dream in which you complete a difficult job points straight toward wealth sufficient to enable you to retire from business.

**COMPLEXION.** It is lucky to dream that your complexion suits you.

**CONCERT.** Good business is foretold to one who dreams of being at a high class concert; also profit from professional work.

**CONFECTIONERY** (*See* Candy).

172

CONFIRMATION. A young person who dreams of being a candidate at this church service will rise to a position of honor and trust.

CONFLAGRATION (*See* Fire).

CONSCIENCE. If your conscience pricks you in a dream, it is a sign that you need not worry about something that you may have considered wrong.

CONVICTION. Dreaming of being convicted for a misdemeanor or crime is usually a prelude to a fortunate occurrence.

COPPER. This metal is a lucky dream. Giving copper pennies to children presages the recovery of lost property.

CORNS. You will be lucky in business if you dream of having to limp on account of corns on your feet.

CORONATION. Seeing a king or queen crowned in a dream is a forerunner of meeting someone of wealth and station who will advance your interests.
   To dream of being a part of coronation ceremonies predicts the acquisition of wealth.

CORPULENCE. If you dream of being very corpulent, the prediction is that you will lead a comfortable life both in body and mind.

COTTAGE. Dreaming of living quietly in a cottage is the prelude to lasting contentment.

COTTON. Whether growing, in bales, in cloth, or clothing, cotton is a dream that foretells wealth. Absorbent cotton, such as used for surgical purposes, augurs good health.

COUGHING. To dream of coughing is to be assured that your health will improve if there is anything the matter with you.

COW. It is good luck to dream of one or more cows. The prediction is of peaceful and profitable pursuits.

COWSLIPS. Dreaming that you see these flowers in bloom is a presage of happiness derived from friendship.

CRADLE. A cradle holding a lovely baby is a portent of much happiness in family life.

CREAM. This dream predicts profit to everyone except the dairyman or farmer.
Drinking cream is a forerunner of good health and prosperity.

CROCKERY. To dream of owning much crockery prophesies gradually increasing financial stability. In whatever form, unless it is broken, and of whatever description, crockery is a fortunate thing to dream about.

CROCUS. This early spring flower is a lucky omen.

CROUP. Health and peace in the home are foretold by a dream of your child being afflicted with croup.

CROWD. A group of people behaving in an orderly fashion betokens sufficient prosperity to make life pleasantly exciting.

CRYING. To dream of hearing someone crying is a portent of good news.
To dream of crying oneself foretells success in an important undertaking.

CUCUMBER. Good health is indicated by a dream of this vegetable, either on the vine or on the table.

CUPBOARD. If it is well stocked with food, dishes and other supplies. the cupboard is a good omen to those who are contemplating an investment or making a change.

**CURB.** It is considered a sign of good luck to step on a curb.

**CURLS.** To dream of your own or someone else's curls is a presage of an improvement in your personal affairs.

## D

**DAHLIAS.** Good fortune in money matters is foretold by a dream of these flowers, especially if they are growing out of doors.

**DAIRY.** Thrift will make you rich if you dream of being in a dairy, either as a worker or an onlooker.

**DAIRYMAID.** Good health and contentment is the promise of a dream in which a dairymaid is seen at work.

**DAISIES.** To dream of walking through a field of daisies, white or yellow, predicts great joy in the near future through the acquisition of something you have always wanted.

**DANCING.** If you dream of seeing white-haired men and women dancing, your financial condition will improve considerably.

To dream of dancing yourself means sudden good fortune.

**DANGER.** Success is foretold by a dream of being in danger.

**DARNING.** Mending socks or other hosiery is a prediction of making a new and valuable friend.

**DATES.** It is a sign of approaching prosperity to see dates growing on a tree.

**DEAFNESS.** If you dream that you are deaf, you will solve a problem that has been disturbing you greatly.

DEBTS. It is a good omen to dream of paying your debts.

DECK. Standing, sitting, or walking on the deck of a ship, either under sail or power, is a fortunate dream if the sea is calm. It predicts that you will make a valuable discovery.

DECORATING. Dreaming that you decorate a house, room, or clothing for a festive occasion, presages happy and lighthearted times.

DEER. To see deer in their native environment is a lucky dream for those who are about to embark on a new enterprise.

DEW. A dream of seeing drops of dew sparkling in the grass or on flowers is an augury of innocent and profitable pleasure.

DIAMONDS. These gems seen or worn in a dream foretell a sufficient income to provide not only the necessities but the luxurious refinements as well.

DIGGING. If hard work that brings success is lucky, then a dream of digging is worth while. A person who has this dream may be assured that his or her efforts will lead slowly but surely to a desired goal.

DIRT. Black pulverized dirt seen in a flower garden is a favorable sign to those who are planning to enter upon a new business enterprise.

DISAPPOINTMENT. The opposite may be expected if you dream of being disappointed in some project in which you are engaged.

DISGRACE. This is another dream which implies the opposite. It signifies honor.

176

**DISHES** (*See* Crockery). Good luck may be confidently expected from a dream of having clean and well arranged dishes. The luck will hold in both financial and personal matters.

**DISMISSED.** To dream of being dismissed or fired from a job is an augury of an increase in salary or an elevation in the position you hold.

**DISPUTES.** This dream portends that you will overcome the obstacles that seem to be hindering your progress.

**DISTRESS.** A dream that points toward success in an undertaking that has appeared to be hopeless.

**DITCH.** If you jump over a ditch, the dream is a good sign. It is a presage of escaping danger of some sort.

**DIVING.** To dream of seeing young men and women diving gracefully into deep water is an omen of pleasant companionship with those you love.
   If you yourself are diving without great effort, the prediction is of an achievement that will gain you many friends.

**DIVIDENDS.** Receiving dividends in a dream presages an increase in your salary or other income.

**DOCTOR.** It is good luck to dream of meeting a doctor socially. If he or she is young and handsome, it is a sign that you will make money in a business venture. If he is old and gray, you will make fortunate social contacts.

**DOG-SHOW.** A renewal of an old and valued friendship will follow a dream of attending a dog-show.

**DOME.** If in your dream, you are climbing either the inside or outside of the dome of a church or other building, the prediction is of a rise in fortune.

DONKEY. To dream of leading a donkey by a halter, it is an indication that you will achieve success through your qualities of leadership.

A white donkey is a most propitious dream. It points to the making or inheritance of a fortune that you will use to your own spiritual benefit and that of your friends.

DOVES. A dream of a dove-cote with many of the doves hovering near is an augury of peace and plenty in the home.

DRAMA. You will meet an old and pleasant friend if you dream of being at the performance of a drama.

DRESS. A woman who dreams of wearing a new and pretty dress will realize her social ambitions.

DRINKING. For a person to dream of drinking water, lemonade, gingerale, or another soft drink while others are indulging in hard liquor is a sign that his or her personality will be of great advantage.

DRIVING. To dream of driving a motor car smoothly along pleasant highways is an augury of good fortune. Driving a carriage behind a horse along a dirt road is a lucky portent if the horse behaves.

DROPS. Using a dropper to measure out medicine is a prediction of a small legacy.

DRUGSTORE. Your speculations will turn out favorably if you dream of entering or working in a drugstore.

DRUMS. Heard in a dream, the sharp, staccato beat of drums is a forerunner of the successful outcome of plans that have been made over a long period.

DUCKS. Wild ducks flying indicate a change for the better. Tame ducks swimming on the surface of a pond predicts freedom from family worries.

**DRAWER.** An open drawer is a good sign. It is better if it seems to be full of clean clothing.

**DUNGHILL.** Profit, either through business, investments or marriage, is indicated by this dream. It foretells bumper crops for the farmer.

**DWARF.** Health and a prosperous year are predicted if you dream of little men and women.

**DYNAMO.** A dynamo, or even a small electric generator, seen in a dream is a portent of pleasant happenings to come in the near future.

## E

**EAGLE.** Lucky is he or she who dreams of an eagle that is alive. To see one soaring above a lonely place is a sign of pleasantly and honestly acquired wealth.

Nesting eagles are a portent of appointment to a position of trust that you will fill with admirable success.

Fighting eagles are an omen that you will be able to clear yourself of an accusation of wrong doing.

To hear an eagle scream augurs well for the success of a musician or other artist. Such will achieve distinction in their profession.

It is also a good sign for those active in politics.

**EARRINGS.** Cheering news is in store for you if you dream of a beautiful woman wearing earrings. If the wearer is plain, you will win a small sum of money.

**EATING** (*See also* separate articles of food). To dream of eating in company with one or more congenial people is, in general, a sign that your lot will be one of contentment.

**EAVESDROPPING.** Listening in secretly on a conversation not meant for your ears is a fortunate augury for those who are planning a change in their business. The chances are all in favor of its being successful.

**EEL.** Grasping an eel in a dream is a good omen if the fish does not wiggle out of your hand.

**EGGS.** Fresh eggs augur success in any enterprise you may start.

To dream of finding fresh laid eggs in a nest is a portent of financial ease.

**ELECTION.** If you dream of working for the election of someone to a public office, you are on the way to some great achievement.

**ELEPHANT.** A lucky dream, whether seen singly or in groups.

Performing elephants are an omen of a happy family life.

Elephants at work foretell prosperity in business.

**ELEVATOR.** It foretells a slow but steady rise in fortune if you dream of ascending swiftly in an elevator. If the elevator goes up slowly, the prophecy is a sudden advancement.

**ELM.** An elm tree that is free from insect pests is an augury of a life of ease.

**EMERALD.** This dream predicts an inheritance that may or may not be advantageous.

**ENTERTAINMENT.** To dream of enjoying an entertainment is a presage of happy times in the near future and of good health for yourself and family.

**ENVY.** A dream of envying another for his material possessions is lucky, but is a forerunner of excellent fortune if one envies another for this disposition.

**ERMINE.** High honors for an achievement may be expected from a dream of this costly fur.

**ERRAND.** If you are sent on a simple errand in a dream, it is prophetic of successful accomplishment.

**ERUPTION.** To dream that your skin has broken out with an eruption is a prophecy that you will gain the confidence of influential people who will look out for your interests.

**ESCAPE.** To escape from danger in a dream, whether it is physical or financial, augurs well for your prospects in business.

**ESTATE.** If in your dream you are the winner of a beautiful large estate, your prospects are unusually bright.

**EVERGREENS.** Money will come to you easily if you dream of evergreen trees or bushes of any kind.

**EXCHANGING.** To dream of exchanging articles of any description is significant to those engaged in business. It foretells profitable deals.

**EXPEDITION.** Whoever dreams of going on an expedition will find that his efforts to better himself will be rewarded.

**EXTRAVAGANCE.** If you dream of paying more for an article than you can possibly afford, it is an augury of happiness within the home circle.

**EYES.** An improvement in your financial condition is foretold by a dream of seeing eyes that have no special connection with any known face.

### F

**FACE.** Pleasant faces seen in a dream are a portent of joyful news from an old friend.

**FAILURE.** To fail in a dream is a sign that you will accomplish the end for which you are working.

**FAIR.** As the word would imply, this dream indicates a fair prospect. To be at a fair augurs well for your material future.

**FAIRY.** Success in spite of all that may seem against it is prophesied by a dream of the fairies that Peter Pan believed in.

**FAITHLESS.** If you dream that someone has been faithless to you, it foretells that your friends will be loyal to you.

**FAKE.** To dream of buying anything that turns out to be a fake is a prediction of a successful business deal.

**FALSEHOOD.** It is fortunate to dream that someone tells you a lie.

**FAMILY.** A large and happy family seen in a dream is an omen of family happiness.
A family of animals seen in their natural environment portends profit in your business.

**FAN.** Good news from an unusual source is predicted by dreaming of a man using a fan.

**FARM.** Prosperity and good health are foretold by a dream of living and working on a farm. If it is a stock or dairy farm, your investments will turn out well.

**FAT** (*See* Corpulence).

**FATIGUE.** An ambition that you have had for a long time will be realized if you dream of being tired after working either at physical or mental labor.

**FAVOR.** To ask a favor in a dream presages your doing a favor for someone who will repay you in a very agreeable manner.

**FAWN.** True friendship is indicated by a dream of a fawn.

**FEATHERS.** The significance of this dream lies chiefly in their color.

Eagle feathers predict that you will achieve the goal of your ambitions.

Ostrich plumes portend a successful business deal.

**FEEDING.** It is lucky to dream of feeding a baby, for it augurs a happy family life.

Feeding animals portends an interesting journey.

**FENCE.** Climbing a fence in a dream is a forerunner of conquering an obstacle.

Building a fence is a sign that you will amass a fortune through industry and commercial genius.

**FERNS.** A lush bed of ferns seen in a dream are prophetic of a release from forebodings of a sinister import.

**FERRY.** A calm crossing of a river, lake or other body of water on a ferry is an omen of the successful working out of a distressing problem.

**FIGHT.** To dream that you win a fight means that you will overcome obstacles.

**FIGS.** It is good luck to see figs growing, for you will have a fortunate and profitable experience.

**FIRE.** This dream is a fortunate one provided the dreamer does not get burned. A happy family life is portended to those who dream that their homes are burning.

Building a fire out of doors, or in a stove or furnace is a sign of coming prosperity.

**FISH.** You will have good fortune if you dream of seeing fish swimming in a stream, particularly trout.

**FLAGS.** The flag of your nation seen in a dream is an omen of prosperity. Other flags must be interpreted through a reference to their predominating colors.

**FLAX.** Growing flax denotes a new enterprise in which you will suceed handsomely.

**FLOATING.** This predicts a victory over an obstacle that has heretofore baffled you.

**FLUTE.** You meet an old friend for whom you have a great liking if you hear a flute being played. It also portends financial gain.

**FOREST.** It is a good omen, signifying pecuniary gain and much joy of life, to dream of many trees bearing green leaves. People who write for a living, or follow one of the other arts, will hear profitable news.

**FORM.** Seeing a beautiful form, whether human or otherwise, portends happiness through congenial occupations.

**FOUNTAIN.** Clear sparkling water shooting high into the air foretells the realization of your highest ambitions.

**FOX.** If you kill a fox in your dream, you will be fortunate in speculative investments.

**FOXGLOVES.** These flowers portend an interesting and agreeable experience.

**FRAGRANCE.** A pleasing new acquaintance is predicted by dreaming of a sweet odor.

**FRAUD.** If you dream of committing a fraud, the indications are all toward a successful and honorable deal.

**FRECKLES.** You will be admired and sought for your cheerful and sunny disposition if you dream of seeing freckles on someone else's face or hands.

**FRIENDS.** To dream of having friends is one of the best

portents that a dream may have.

If you dream of helping a friend with money, you will be both happy and prosperous.

FRIGHT. A sudden fright is a forerunner of a calm period of life in easy circumstances.

FROGS. Good business prospects are predicted by a dream of frogs sunning themselves on lily pads.

If the frogs jump into the water, it signifies a new enterprise that will turn out to your advantage.

To hear frogs is a sign of contentment in the home and among friends.

FROWN. It is an omen of domestic happiness if a man dreams of seeing his wife or children frowning. The same is true for a wife.

FRUIT. In general, it is an augury of success to dream of eating fruit if it is ripe, juicy and of good flavor.

FURNACE (*See* Fire).

FURS. Luxurious furs, either on yourself or another, denote an improvement in your income, either through marriage, investments or an increase in salary.

## G

GAIN. To dream of making a gain is a sign of relief from a worry that may be oppressing you.

GAITERS. Wearing gaiters presages pleasing news from a source you have all but forgotten.

GALE. If a gale seems to be blowing in a dream, it is an indication that the portent of the rest of the dream will be increased in its good luck features.

GALLOPING. To be astride a galloping horse on a straight

road foretells the achievement of your plans for bettering yourself. This is an even better dream if the horse is piebald.

GAMES. Playing games in a dream is generally a good sign if there is no reference to whether you are winning or losing. Games of skill have a better chance, and outdoor games of an athletic nature are best of all.

GARDEN. A dream of a lovely garden, whether large or small, is a portent of peaceful pursuits in good company: and of no financial worries.

GARLIC. (*See* Onions).

GASOLINE. To dream of having your automobile tank filled with gasoline predicts a journey that will be profitable both in pleasure and finance.

GEESE. Walking along a grassy lane, a flock of geese portend an event which will be fortunate so far as your business affairs are concerned.

GHOST. To dream of being friendly with a ghost is an excellent portent. Your industry will win honor and riches for you.

GIFT. To dream of making a gift to a friend or an institution is the forerunner of a profitable business deal.

GIRLS. A pretty, wholesome, innocent girl seen in a dream foretells happiness through upright living.

GLEANERS. To see gleaners in a field of wheat or rye predicts successful business dealings with your fellow men.

GLOVES. Wearing gloves in a dream is practically a guarantee of coming prosperity.

**GOATS.** These animals grazing in an open space are an augury of good fortune.

**GOLD.** As might be expected, it is fortunate to dream of this precious metal. The prediction is of wealth, honors, long life, or happiness—or combination of any or all of these.

**GOLDFISH.** This is a fortunate dream, if the goldfish are swimming either in a pool or bowl, especially for someone who is planning to go on the stage or into the movies.

**GOLF.** To dream of making a good score in golf is indicative of business success.

**GOOSEBERRIES.** It is an augury of improvement in both one's family affairs and business prospects to dream of eating ripe gooseberries.

**GRAIN.** In the field, harvested, or in storage bins, grain is a dream of fortunate import.

**GRANDPARENT.** If you dream of being a grandparent, your prospects of family happiness are distinctly favorable.

To dream of one or more grandparents is a sign that you will succeed through the exercise of tact.

**GRAPES** (*See* Fruit).

**GRASS.** Green grass is always a good omen in connection with any enterprise in which you may be engaged.

**GRATITUDE.** It is lucky to dream of showing gratitude to God or friends for favors received.

**GREYHOUND.** This animal portends that you will achieve your aim in competition with others who may seem to have superior qualifications.

**GUITAR.** To dream of playing this instrument denotes ease in your future life with many friends of real substance.

**GULLS.** These birds soaring over the water are an indication of auspicious happenings in your immediate future. If they alight it foretells a legacy that may or may not be expected.

# H

**HAIR.** It is a fortunate omen to dream of finding a hair when cutting a piece of butter if it does not disgust you.

Being pleased with the appearance of your hair foretells that you will take a trip to a distant city under exceptionally favorable circumstances.

To dream of mussing someone else's hair is a sign that you will inherit a small sum of money.

**HAIRPINS.** Finding hairpins on the floor presages an unusual and pleasing experience.

To repair a broken piece of machinery with a hairpin is an indication that you will receive a gift of some kind.

**HANDS.** If the hands are clean, well-kept and capable looking, the augury is of happiness and easy living.

It is good luck to dream of shaking hands, especially with someone of a higher station in life. Holding hands with one of the opposite sex foretells financial stability.

**HANGING.** A dream of being hanged for a crime is a fortunate augury for those who have a business deal in process.

**HARLOT.** For a man to dream of visiting a harlot is a sign that he will inherit money from someone who made it in a dubious manner.

**HARVEST.** This is a prediction of plentiful returns on an investment which you had believed worthless.

**HAT.** If the hat is new, smart and becoming, the portent is favorable. After such a dream is an auspicious time to begin a new enterprise.

**HATE.** To dream that anyone hates you is a sign that someone will do you a favor.

**HAWK.** If you kill or capture this bird of prey, the dream is a favorable one.

**HEARTH** (*See* Home). A hearth with a cheerful fire burning is a dream which means relief from nervous or other tension.

**HEDGES.** If green and neatly trimmed, hedges are an augury of a well-ordered life.

**HELL.** A dream of the conventional hell, with fire and brimstone, devils with pitchforks, and other traditional paraphernalia, is a forerunner of an amusing experience.

**HEN.** A brooding hen or a hen laying an egg is an omen of pleasure at meeting an old friend.

**HIGH SCHOOL.** If you dream of attending high school, you are likely to have an honor conferred upon you.

**HOBBY.** In general it is lucky to dream of pursuing a hobby such as photography, stamp collecting, or similar diversions that do not involve the taking of life.

**HOECAKE.** To dream of eating hoecake indicates a long period of prosperity.

**HOME.** If a dream of home is one that is pleasant and cheerful, it is a portent of the coming of a visitor whose presence will be a great advantage.

**HOMINY.** An important letter may be expected after a dream of eating this food.

**HOUSE.** Building a house, or causing one to be built, predicts a long and happy family life.

**HUMMING BIRD.** If it is on the wing, the humming bird is a fortunate dream for those who enjoy travel to distant places.

**HYMNS.** Hearing or singing sacred songs in a dream is an augury of lasting contentment.

# I

**ICE CREAM.** Popularity among people of both sexes is foretold by a dream of eating this dessert.

**IMPS** (*See* Hell). An unusual event of importance with a humorous turn is predicted by this dream.

**INCENSE.** If it has an agreeable odor, incense foretells an increase in luxury.

**INCOME.** To dream of a dwindling income betokens a raise in salary for a wage-earner.

**INFANT.** To see a newborn infant in a dream prophesies that with care one may avoid a great difficulty.

**INN.** To be taking your ease in an inn is a dream that betokens a vacation from worry.

**INSANITY.** This is a dream of lucky import, whether it is yourself or someone else who is afflicted.

**INVENTOR.** If you dream of inventing a new device, or of working on an invention, you will be able to carry out an important project.

**ITCH.** It is a sign that you will be left a valuable piece of property if you dream that your buttocks itch.

If one hand itches you will meet a stranger.
If your eye itches you will receive money.

## J

JACKASS (*See* Donkey). To dream of "making an ass of oneself" portends an invitation to a party where you will meet influential people.

JADE (*See* Color). Ornaments of this beautiful stone are a lucky portent, especially if the color is green.

JEWELS. Financial good fortune may be confidently expected if you dream of seeing or wearing jewels.

JINGLE. To hear jingling bells or coins is a forerunner of a small bequest from a distant relative.

JILT. You will be fortunate if you dream of being jilted by a lover.

JOCKEY. Dreaming of a jockey riding a horse in a race is a presage of unexpected good fortune.

JOURNEY. A dream of a pleasant journey is a joyful augury. It denotes a change in your life that will work out for the better.

JOY. Continuous good health is predicted by a dream if you feel happiness.

JUBILEE. If in your dream you attend a jubilee, your success as a leader is assured.

JUG. To dream of drinking liquor from a jug predicts that you will be lucky in the next lottery for which you buy a ticket.

JUGGLER. An increase in your financial resources will follow a dream of seeing a juggler keep a number of articles in the air. The more articles there are, the better is the augury.

JUMPING. If you dream of jumping over a chair or other piece of furniture, you will overcome a serious obstacle.

JUNIPER. To taste the flavor of juniper in your dream is a prelude to pleasant diversions.

## K

KEEPSAKE. Without reference to its value, a keepsake received in a dream is a forerunner of good fortune to those who are married or who are planning to be.

KETTLE. A bright, shiny kettle of copper or tin is a pleasant augury for married folk.

KICK. It is a good omen, particularly in business affairs, to kick someone else in your dream.

KIDNAPING. If you dream of a kidnaping of some famous person, it presages the inheritance of a small sum of money.

KISSING. This is a dream which depends on the innocence of the kiss for its predictions. If it is someone whom you have a right to kiss, the dream portends high honors and a comfortable living.

KITE. To dream of successfully flying a kite is a look forward to the acquisition of wealth; the higher the flight, the greater the wealth.

KNIFE. A surgeon's knife is an augury of an improvement in health through the removal of a diseased part.

KNITTING. This is a fortunate dream, for it signifies domestic felicity from now on.

**KNOT.** It is a prophecy of the happy solution of a perplexing problem if you dream of untying a knot in a rope or string.

# L

**LABEL.** To label any package or container in a dream foretells a pleasant surprise.

**LABOR.** It predicts an increase in your income if you dream of doing manual labor, especially if it appears to be tiresome or painful.

**LACE.** If the lace seen or worn in a dream seems to be handmade or of fine quality, the augury is such that you may look forward to an easy life.

**LADDER.** To dream of climbing a ladder predicts success in any new enterprise.

**LADY.** A naked lady seen in a dream is a fortunate augury if the circumstances are not scandalous.

**LAKE.** The condition of the lake and weather govern the import of this dream. If both are calm, the omen is exceedingly fortunate.

**LAMBS.** It is a happy augury if you dream of lambs grazing or gamboling in open sunlit spaces. It foretells success and happiness.

**LAMPS.** Good business may be confidently expected if you dream of lighted lamps, whether they are gas, electric or oil.

**LAND.** To dream of owning land is a sign of coming prosperity.

　　If you see land from the deck of a steamer, it foretells a successful business deal.

**LANTERN.** Lighting your pathway with a lantern of any kind points toward a solution of your most pressing problems.

**LAP.** One may expect ease of mind if he or she dreams of sitting in the lap of another.

**LAP-ROBE.** To dream of holding hands with someone of the opposite sex under a lap-robe is a sign that your trust in human nature will bring you great honor.

**LARD.** You will put to shame anyone who has been an irritation to you if you dream of using lard.

**LARK.** The song of the lark heard in a dream presages a happy, carefree life.

**LAUGHING.** This dream depends on the spirit of the laughter. If it is in pure fun, and not at someone's discomfiture, it augurs freedom from worry.

**LAUREL.** One may reasonably expect a sizable sum of money if he or she dreams of this lovely wild plant.

**LAVENDER.** Either growing, or merely as a fragrance, lavender portends sterling friendship in time of stress.

**LAWN.** It is a fortunate augury to dream of strolling on a velvety green lawn, denoting ease and contentment.

**LEAPING** (*See* Jumping).

**LEARNING.** If the knowledge gained is of a practical nature, it is an omen of business improvement to dream of learning something new.
   Professional men and women will profit in their own lines after a dream of abstract learning.

**LEASE.** You have every reason to expect a valuable gift if you dream of leasing a house, office, or other piece of property.

**LEAVES.** Leaves if they are green, are generally a good augury, whether in business, family life or other pursuits.

**LEDGER.** Good luck will follow a dream of balancing a ledger account.

**LEFT-HANDED.** It is a sign of popularity if you dream or yourself or another being left-handed.

To dream of seeing a left-handed pitcher or batter in a baseball game portends a successful business deal.

To dream of a right-handed person trying to write with the left hand, or vice-versa, is very lucky in its augury.

**LEGS.** Beautiful legs on one of the opposite sex seen in a dream are a portent of a new acquaintance who will prove to be a valuable friend.

**LESSONS.** It is a sign that you are to begin a successful enterprise if you dream of taking lessons in some worthy subject.

**LIBEL.** If you dream that you are libeled and that you resent it, you are on the way to some outstanding business success.

**LICENSE.** Getting either an automobile or dog license in a dream predicts surprising and profitable news from an unexpected source.

**LIGHT.** To dream of being grateful for a light, either in a dark place or for a cigarette or cigar, denotes relief from an embarrassing situation.

**LIGHTNING.** Whether sheet or chain lightning, this dream foretells a sudden and pronounced improvement in your affairs.

**LINEN.** This is a good dream for those who enjoy wearing fine clothes, for it predicts sufficient income to indulge this taste to the limit.

**LION OR LIONESS.** In its habitat, the lion is an augury of personal success and high standing in the community.

**LIQUOR.** To drink liquor in a dream foretells business success.

**LIVER.** It is a sign that you will enjoy good health if you dream of eating liver.

A dream of your own liver indicates that you will develop your own personality to advantage.

**LIVERY.** If you dream of having servants in livery it is an indication of an improvement in your affairs.

**LOBSTER** (*See* Color). The significance of a lobster dream depends on its color—red when cooked, and green when alive.

**LOCOMOTIVE.** This is a dream of good fortune. You will go far in your chosen field of work.

**LOTTO.** It presages pleasant hours spent in the company of persons whom you like.

**LYRE.** This ancient stringed instrument, heard in a dream, is a forerunner of happy hours spent in agreeable company.

## M

**MACHINERY.** Smoothly running machinery is an augury of a normal and well ordered family life in a pleasant community.

**MAGAZINE.** It depends on how the magazine affects you in your dream whether or not the omen is good. If its contents, illustrations and make-up give you pleasure, you will have a profitable experience.

**MAGNET.** To dream of a magnet indicates that you will

make one or more new friends who will prove a blessing.

**MALICE.** It augurs well for your success in business if you dream that someone shows malice toward you.

**MALT.** Domestic bliss is foretold by a dream of malt.

**MANGLE.** A woman who dreams of ironing clothes on a mangle will be fortunate in her social relations.

**MANICURE.** To dream of having one's fingernails attended to by a manicurist is a sign of coming distinction.

**MANUFACTURING.** It is an excellent sign for those about to embark in a new business if they dream of manufacturing.

**MANURE.** This is a lucky dream, for it presages enrichment through hard work.

**MANUSCRIPT.** If you dream of having your manuscript rejected by a publisher, it augurs success in the profession of writing.

**MARKET.** A market of any kind, except those of shameful import, is a good sign for those who plan an ocean trip.

**MASON.** To dream of seeing a mason laying bricks predicts social advancement that leads by degrees to a well-established financial condition.

**MATCHES.** You will receive money if you dream of matches. If you strike a match, the money will come suddenly.

**MAYPOLE.** If you dream of dancing around a maypole, it is a prediction of great happiness to come.

**MEADOW.** A pleasant meadow betokens calm pleasures in the company of people whom you admire and respect.

MECHANIC. You will receive some sort of promotion after having this dream. It predicts something constructive.

MEDALS. To dream of wearing medals is a forerunner of a season of merrymaking.

MELODY. Sweet music heard in a dream predicts business success.

MILK. Drinking milk in a dream is a portent of excellent health.
   Selling milk is an omen of a comfortable income.
   Bathing in milk is a forecast of pleasure in life.

MILLS (*See* Manufacturing).

MISFORTUNE. This dream cannot be definitely interpreted as it is too general. Look up references to specific misfortunes.

MISTLETOE. Growing on a tree, mistletoe signifies that you will always have a friend in need.
   A dream of kissing under a sprig of mistletoe predicts a carefree existence.

MOCKING BIRD. An improvement in your finances is imminent if you dream of hearing one of these birds sing.

MONEY. To give, lend or pay money is an augury that you will receive a large sum in a surprising manner.
   If you dream of handling other people's money and resist the temptation to steal it, you will inherit something of value from a relative.

MOON. A new moon seen in a dream foretells commercial success and pleasant friends.

**MOSQUITOES.** It is good luck to dream of killing one or more of these pests.

**MOTHER** (*See* Mother-in-law). This is always a favorable dream. It is an omen that you will gain the esteem of the world through your uprightness.

**MOTOR CAR.** To dream of riding along a fine highway in a luxurious motor car indicates that you will make a large amount of money through a business deal or invention that at first seemed unimportant.

**MOUNTAIN.** To reach the summit of a mountain after a long and difficult climb is a dream that presages ultimate success in writing, painting, or on the stage and screen.

**MOVING PICTURES.** This depends on the character of the exhibition. the omen usually follows the suggestion of the action seen on the screen.

**MOWING** (*See* Harvest). It is an indication of general good fortune if you dream of running a lawn mower or mowing machine.

**MUFF.** It is a sign that you will be protected against misfortune if you dream of wearing a muff.

**MUSIC** (*See* Melody). To dream of hearing music that is melodious or inspiring is a forerunner of success in an enterprise that is carried on with the accompaniment of great noise.

**MUSTARD.** Mustard blossoms seen in a dream foretell an interesting life in the future.

# N

**NAPKINS.** Of whatever description, napkins foretell surprising but pleasant news.

NAVY. You will overcome your greatest difficulties if you dream of your own country's navy; one ship or many are lucky, but the greater the number, the better the omen.

NECK. It predicts the receipt of a sum of money to dream that you have a stiff neck.

NEGATIVES. Photographic negatives, whether of glass or film, are an indication that you will escape an accident or sickness.

NEGRO. It denotes a favorable turn in your affairs if you dream of seeing a negro in comfortable surroundings.

NEST. Bird's nests are fortunate augury as to home arrangements.

NEWSPAPERS. Reading a newspaper in a dream is good luck if the news is very exciting or distressing.

NEW YEAR. A change for the better in both your personal and business relations is portended by a dream of New Year's Day or New Year's Eve.

NICKNAME. To hear your nickname used in a dream is an omen of new and agreeable friends.

NIGHTINGALE. The song of this bird heard in a dream is a presage of wholesome pleasures and moderate prosperity.

NOSEBLEED. This augurs health and relief from anxiety.

NUGGET. To dream of finding a nugget of gold or other precious metal predicts an elevation above your present position.

NUTS. Prosperity will follow a dream of gathering or eating nuts from trees.
    If you dream of screwing a nut on a bolt, it is a sign that you will achieve a new ambition.

NYMPH. A dream of lovely nymphs bathing in a woodland pool foretells the realization of desires for rich and sumptuous living.

## O

OAK. This sturdy tree in a dream is a splendid augury of solid success in your most important undertakings.

To see acorns dropping from an oak tree indicates a fortunate sudden turn in business.

To use oak in building foretells enduring prosperity.

OARS. To dream of propelling a boat with oars shows that you will succeed through hard work.

OATS. A ripening field of oats is a sign of business and social success.

OCEAN. A calm ocean in your dream foretells peaceful pursuits.

ODOR. Inhaling a pleasant odor is an omen of improved business conditions.

OFFSPRING. To dream of your own offspring is a presage of the sudden acquisition of money.

OLIVES. Eating ripe olives is a forerunner of unusual pleasures.

OMNIBUS. Popularity among your fellow men is predicted by a dream of riding on an omnibus. If you ride on top, the augury is even better.

ONIONS. This and other vegetables of a similar nature, such as garlic, are prophetic that your vigorous attention to business will result in satisfactory rewards.

ORANGES. Ripe oranges seen on a tree presage financial gain.

**ORCHARD.** An orchard well laden with ripe fruit is a dream that is considered generally lucky by every authority on dream interpretation.

**ORCHESTRA** (*See* Melody, Music). To dream of hearing an orchestra playing music that is harmonious and inspiring is a prediction of just that kind of life.

**ORGAN** (*See* Melody, Music, Orchestra). The kind of music you hear from this instrument controls the prediction of the dream.

**ORNAMENT.** Honors are foretold by a dream of wearing ornaments or of ornamenting a house or room.

**OUTBOARD MOTOR.** To dream of having a boat propelled by an outboard motor denotes a rapid improvement in your career through hard work.

**OVERALLS.** It is a forerunner of general luck if you dream of wearing overalls.

**OXEN.** Good fortune is foretold by a dream of well-conditioned oxen at work on the road or in the field.

To dream of driving a yoke of oxen means that you will make a success of any new enterprise in which you may embark.

### P

**PAGODA.** A pleasant journey, either in your own country or abroad, is predicted by a dream of a Chinese or other pagoda.

**PAIN.** To dream of being in pain is a presage of ease and contentment.

**PAINTER.** It is a sign of an improvement in your condition, both of health and finance, to dream of seeing a painter at work. The painter may be painting a house, fence, sign, or a picture; the omen is the same in each instance.

PALACE. If your dream is of living in a palace, with many luxuries, the augury is that you are on the way to making much money.

PALM TREE. This is a dream of a strange situation that will work out for your own good.

PARADISE. To dream of Paradise predicts a meeting with a stranger who will turn out to be a worthy friend.

PARASOL. An open parasol out of doors is a sign of fair prospects for your every day life.

PARENTS. It predicts some unusual form of happiness to dream of both your parents at the same time.

PARK. Being in a well-kept park with someone you like points toward a future with few pressing problems.

PARTRIDGES. It is an auspicious time to begin a new enterprise if you dream of seeing a covey of partridges.

PARTY. To dream of being at a gay and pleasant party is an augury of an agreeable existence.

PATCH. If in a dream your clothes appear to be patched, it is a sign that you will inherit money.

PAYING. The payment of bills, debts and loans in a dream is a fortunate augury for those who owe money.

PEARLS. Collecting pearls in a dream foretells that your business genius will win large rewards for you.

PEAS. Health and prosperity are predicted by a dream of eating green peas.

PENCIL. Useing a pencil in a dream foretells that you will

be called upon to sign a document that will bring large profits.

PEPPER. Your children will succeed in enterprises, either business or professional, if you dream of eating or handling pepper.

PERFUME (See Odor).

PIANO (See Melody, Music, Orchestra, Organ). As with other musical instruments, the significance of a dream of hearing a piano is good or not according to the tunefulness of the music.

PHOTOGRAPHY. It is a sign of future contentment to dream of working with photography as a hobby.

PHYSICIAN. Good health is in store for you if you dream of seeing a physician either professionally or personally.

PICNIC. Dreaming of a pleasant time at a picnic is an augury of the solution of a perplexing problem.

PIGEON (See Dove.).

PILLOW. It is a sign of ease if you dream of laying your head on a soft pillow.

PILLS. Taking pills in a dream is a prediction of success in a business deal.

PINAFORE. A dream of a child wearing a pinafore foretells simple pleasures that will give much happiness and lead to greater comfort in life.

PINE TREE. It is an augury of steadfastness on the part of your friends if you dream of this evergreen.

PIPE. To dream of smoking tobacco in a pipe is an omen of a calm attitude toward whatever may befall.

PLAY (*See* Actor). If the play seen in a dream is pleasing, the import is some achievement which, though it may be small, will give much pleasure.

POETRY. To dream of writing poetry is a forerunner of a letter that will bring good news.

POLICE. It is a good sign to dream that a policeman arrests you for a minor infraction of the law.

POND. An even-tempered existence, with a sufficient income, is to be looked for after a dream of a placid pond.

POOL (*See also* Bathing, Nymph, Swimming). A clean, attractive pool, with or without bathers, augurs a surprising occurrence that will work out to your advantage.

POSTAGE STAMPS. It is a sign of remunerative activities to dream of collecting postage stamps as a hobby.

POTATOES. Eating fried potatoes in a dream is a forerunner of being lavishly entertained.

POTTERY. To dream of seeing pottery made is a sign that you will achieve good fortune through skill with plastic materials.

POVERTY. This dream predicts a change for the better in your business.

PRAIRIE. Being on a green prairie in a dream is an augury of general improvement in your condition.

PRICK. To dream of receiving a prick from a needle or other sharp instrument foretells a valuable gift.

PROSTITUTE (*See* Harlot).

**PUBLISHER.** If you dream of a publisher rejecting your manuscript it is a sign that you will succeed in spite of obstacles.

**PUMP.** An old-fashioned pump with a handle that rocks up and down predicts eventual success in your chosen field of occupation.

A pump operated by steam or electricity is a portent of a gift of money that will enable you to carry out your plans.

**PURSE.** A good bank account is foretold by a dream of finding money in your purse.

# Q

**QUAIL** (*See* Partridge).

**QUARREL.** Contrary to what one might expect, it is an omen of good luck in commercial pursuits to dream of having a quarrel.

**QUAY.** A voyage to a foreign land is foretold by a dream of standing on a quay where ships are at rest.

**QUESTION.** It is lucky to ask questions in a dream.

**QUILT.** Improvement in your business conditon and social standing is to be confidently expected after dreaming of a bed quilt.

# R

**RABBITS.** After a dream of rabbits, if they are of normal color, is a good time to start a new business. If they are of unusual hues—such as blue or green—consult colors.

**RACE.** If you win a race in a dream—afoot, horseback, or in an automobile—you will be able to hold your own in competition with others.

**RAINBOW.** A dream of this beautiful natural phenomenon is a harbinger of the "pot of gold" that is said to be found at the rainbow's end.

**RAKE.** To rake grass or leaves in a dream is to be assured of a happy home life.

**RAT.** If in a dream you kill a rat, the augury for business success is excellent. The larger the rat, the better is the augury.

**RECONCILIATION.** Problems that have distressed you will be solved if you dream of a reconciliation with someone whom you have quarreled with.

**REAPERS.** Financial improvement is predicted by a dream of reapers, either hand or machinery, at work in a field.

**RECITING.** If you dream of reciting poetry, you may look forward confidently to social popularity.

**RESCUE.** It is a portent of increasing good fortune to dream of rescuing someone from danger or death. It is better luck if the person is of the opposite sex.

**RESTAURANT.** To dream of eating in a clean, attractive restaurant is a sign that you will have a friend in need.

**RHEUMATISM.** Good health is predicted by a dream of having this painful affliction.

**RHINOCEROS.** This animal predicts that, by patient attention to your present work, you will reach the goal toward which you are aiming. If you dream of killing one, the dream is just that much more auspicious.

**RIDING.** It is a sign of general good fortune to dream that you are riding horseback with one of the opposite sex.

**RING.** Dreaming of wearing a ring, or seeing one on another's hand, foretells financial gains.

**ROBIN.** This bird, seen or heard in a dream, presages hope for better things under the most depressing circumstances.

**ROLLS.** Fresh rolls signify pleasant times to come through an increased understanding of life and its problems.

**ROOF.** To dream of being on a roof is a portent of reaching the top in business. If you are on a roof with one of the opposite sex, you will have social as well as business success.

**ROSARY.** If in your dream you are telling the beads of your rosary, it is a sign that your worries are at an end.

**ROSES.** Fresh, lovely roses of suitable color (*see* Color), growing out of doors or beautifully arranged in bowls or vases, are an omen of the realization of your dearest wishes.

**ROWBOAT.** If the water is calm and the day or evening is fine, to dream of being in a rowboat predicts happy days to come. If you have a pleasant companion of the opposite sex, the augury is especially good.

**RUBBISH.** To dream of rubbish heaps is an omen that your business will improve.

**RUINS.** It is a fortunate augury if you dream of a church or castle in ruins, for it presages the upbuilding of your material resources.

**RUSTLING.** If you dream of the rustling of leaves or of silk, you will receive a communication that will have a salutary effect on your future life, both as regards your material welfare and your standing in the community in which you live.

### S

**SACRIFICE.** A dream of making a sacrifice of any kind is a portent of well-being that is unexpected.

SADDLE. Being in a saddle foretells your rise to a position of authority in business.

To saddle a horse is an augury of the receipt of money that you had given up as hopeless.

SADNESS. This is a contrary dream, for it predicts happiness. To dream of the sadness of someone else is a sign that you will be happy through your ability to help another.

SAFE. To dream of a safe where money is kept augurs a sudden improvement in your financial condition.

SAGE. It is a fortunate omen to dream of seeing or smelling sage. It foretells a new friend who will help you toward the realization of the ambition of your life.

SAILING. If it is on calm waters, your sailing in a dream is a forerunner of achievement.

SALT. Tasting salt in a dream presages an interesting and not unprofitable experience.

SAUSAGE. If you dream of eating sausage of any description, you will be mystified by an occurrence that will eventually work out to your advantage.

SAW. Using a saw in a dream is a fortunate augury if you appear to be making progress. The faster the progress, the better are your chances for success.

SCALD. Future ease is predicted by dreaming of being scalded with hot water or other liquids.

SCARLET (See Color).

SCHOOL. Distinction will come to you if you dream of attending school. It is an augury of progress in many lines.

209

SEA. A calm sea, especially if the sunshine is bright, foretells smooth sailing on the sea of life.

SERENADE. To dream of serenading someone of the opposite sex, or of being serenaded, is a sign of being awarded a prize for some service.

SHABBY. If you dream of being shabby, it portends the ability to buy all the new clothes you may wish.

SHAKING HANDS. To shake hands in a dream is a lucky sign if the person with whom you shake hands is better dressed than you are.

SHAWL. Seeing someone wear a shawl in a dream foretells a new and interesting acquaintance.
Wearing a shawl yourself means that you will be able to do a service that will give you great pleasure.

SHEEP. To dream of a flock of sheep grazing in a green field is a sign of plenty and the ability to make friends.

SHEPHERD. If the shepherd is accompanied by sheep or lambs the sign is the same as for sheep.

SHIRT. Whether you are a man or a woman, it is a fortunate augury to dream of a shirt. Giving away one's shirt is a particularly fortunate sign.

SILK. If you dream of wearing fine silks, you will achieve some secret wish.

SKIDDING. To dream of skidding in an automobile and avoiding accident means that you will be able to avert threatening danger.

SKY. A bright sky, flecked with fleecy clouds, predicts that you will enter upon a period of affluence.

**SMALLPOX.** It is fortunate to dream of having this disease. You will profit in your next business venture.

**SNEEZING.** Good luck comes from sneezing in a dream. it is usually the precursor of health beyond what you have previously enjoyed.

**SNUFF** (*See* Sneezing). If your dream of snuff includes sneezing, it is a fortunate augury.

**SOUP.** Soup in a dream is always a sign that points toward prosperity. If you are eating it and making a prodigious noise, it portends unusual good fortune.

**SPARROWS.** Although these birds are regarded by many as obnoxious, it is a forerunner of good luck if you dream of them. They signify popularity among the people with whom you associate.

**SPEAR.** It foretells the success of your business if you dream of carrying a spear of any kind.

**SPEEDBOAT.** To dream of driving a speedboat is portentous of good tidings in relation to your material welfare.

**SPIDER.** This industrious insect is a presage of success through industry and skill.

**SPOTS.** Spots on your clothing are a prediction that you will be able to pay your bills in full within a short space of time. If you are unsuccessful in trying to remove them, it is an omen of high standing in your community.

**STAMPS.** It is good luck to dream of collecting postage stamps as a hobby.

**STARCH.** To dream of using starch in any way presages that you will succeed through having self-respect.

**STARVING.** If you dream of starving, it is a sign that you will make an oustanding success of the business in which you are engaged.

**STEPS.** To go up steps in a dream means that you will ascend the ladder of fortune. You may expect large returns on any investment you may make.

**STRANGERS.** You will meet new and valuable friends if you dream of coming in contact with strangers.

**STRAWBERRIES.** These berries, eaten or seen, are a presage of unexpected luck. The luck may be concerned with money, or it may be in connection with friends.

**STRUMPET** (*See* Harlot).

**SUGAR.** The import of this dream is as might be expected—a pleasant and easy life in the near future.

**SUNRISE AND SUNSET.** If either of these is brilliant, the augury is good. Happy days are predicted, with freedom from worry.

**SUSPENDERS.** This article of wearing apparel is a sign that when you need help, it will be forthcoming.

**SWIMMING.** If the swimming is without effort and gives pleasure, this dream augurs a smooth and prosperous existence.

**SYMPHONY** (*See also* Melody, Music, Orchestra, Organ, Piano). To dream of a symphony that delights and inspires is a prediction of a realization of your hopes.

## T

**TABLE.** Good times are predicted by a dream of a dining-table set with clean linen and bright silver and glassware.

**TAMBOURINE.** Gayety will come into your life after a

dream of seeing a tambourine or hearing it played.

TAPESTRY. To dream of seeing tapestry of beautiful design and color is to be able to look forward to the rich enjoyment of life.

TARTS. Eating tarts in a dream is a forerunner of small but sure profits in your business.

TASSELS. As a decoration on anything but clothing, tassels are an augury of delight in pleasant companionship.

TAXES. It is significant of good luck in a financial way if you dream of paying taxes.

TEARS. If you dream of crying, you will be confident of happiness.

TEMPTATION. It is a fortunate augury to dream of resisting temptation, especially if it concerns sex.

TENT. Sleeping in a tent, or dreaming of going to bed, is a sign that you will make a friend younger than yourself by reason of your kindness to him or her.

TERRIER. Friendship of many people is betokened by a dream of a terrier of any kind that appears to like you.

THEATRE (*See* Actor, Dancing, Play, Stage).

THIMBLE. For a woman to dream of losing her thimble predicts that she will be prominent among the women of her community.

THREAD. A dream of using thread is a forerunner of acquiring a competency through thrift.

TICKET. Buying a ticket in a dream foretells that you will be lucky in a business venture. The ticket may be for a railroad trip or other transportation, or for a theatre.

**TIMBER.** Either standing or piled in a lumber yard, timber is an augury of an improvement in your financial condition. The odor of pine boards is a particularly good omen.

**TOBACCO.** If you smoke tobacco in a dream, it betokens a release from cares and worries.

**TOMATOES.** This vegetable, eaten in a dream, if it is red ripe, predicts health and prosperity. Look up *Red* under COLOR.

**TORCH.** Seeing a person carrying a torch in a dream is a prediction of a party at which you will have considerable fun.

**TORTURE.** It is fortunate to dream of being tortured, for it presages happiness in your family life.

**TOYS.** To dream of playing with toys is a good sign for married folk. It foretells the success of their children.

**TREES.** In full leaf, trees seen in a dream are a harbinger of contentment through success and good health.

**TRIPLETS** (*See also* Twins, Quadruplets, Quintuplets). Wealth is foretold when anyone dreams of being the parent of triplets.

**TRUNK.** Packing a trunk in a dream is a forerunner of a trip that is likely to have a good effect on your income. To close and lock a trunk augurs good health.

**TWINS.** You will receive a letter that will give you great pleasure if you dream of seeing twins dressed alike.

U

**UDDERS.** It is a sign of plenty to dream of a cow's or goat's udders.

214

**UGLINESS.** A person who is ugly in his or her features seen in a dream is a portent of the inheritance of real estate.

**UMBRELLA.** It is a fortunate omen to dream of carrying an open umbrella in the rain.

**UNFAITHFULNESS.** A dream of the unfaithfulness of your husband, wife or sweetheart indicates that there is no cause for suspicion.

**UNIFORMS.** It is generally an omen of coming prosperity to dream of men or women wearing spotless and well-tailored uniforms.

**URGING.** If in your dream someone is urging you to do something against your will, it is a sign that you will be lucky in speculations.

## V

**VALENTINE.** Receiving a valentine in a dream portends that you will see an old lover under pleasant conditions.

**VASE.** A beautiful vase, especially if it contains flowers, presages contentment in all family relations.

**VELVET.** To see velvet in a dream, whether you are wearing it, or someone else, is usually fortunate, depending on the color. Look up COLOR.

**VERMIN.** If you are afflicted with vermin in a dream, you will receive a letter that will lead to money.

**VIEW.** A lovely view seen in a dream is an omen of release from any vexatious problems that may have been troubling you.

**VILLAGE.** To visit a quiet and charming village in your dream foretells a contented life.

**VINEYARD.** A dream of a vineyard denotes success in your chosen field of endeavor.

**VIOLENCE.** If you are the victim of violence, your life will be calm and moderately successful financially.

To do violence to another in a dream augurs great business success.

**VIRGIN.** A virgin seen in a dream is a portent of success in one of the arts, particularly in such branches as the stage or motion pictures.

**VISITING.** It is fortunate to dream of visiting a relative or friend if the circumstances connected with the visit are pleasant.

**VOICES.** The omen connected with dreaming of voices is good or bad according to whether the voices are pleasant or otherwise. Voices raised in an altercation are sometimes prophetic of profit if one of them seems to favor a just cause.

**VOYAGE.** An inheritance is foretold by a dream of going on a long voyage to a country you do not know.

## W

**WADING.** If wading in a stream or pool gives you pleasure in a dream, the prophecy is of an invitation that you will do well to accept.

**WAGES.** It is an auspicious omen to dream of paying wages. There is a reward somewhere in store for you.

**WAIST.** To put a belt around your waist denotes the solution of a problem of a serious nature.

Putting your arms around the waist of someone of the opposite sex augurs well for your success in commercial transaction.

**WALTZ.** Lasting pleasures will be yours if you dream of waltzing at a dancing party.

**WAREHOUSE.** It is a prophecy of being able to have virtually anything you want to dream of being in a warehouse where goods of many kinds are stored.

**WARTS.** Irritating as they are in real life, warts in dreams are a sign of considerable sums of money that will come to you.

**WATER.** If it is clear and calm, or sparkling, water is a splendid dream for those who are in the business of selling food.

**WATERFALL.** One of the luckiest dreams a person can have. It presages great happiness through an understanding of life, with many friends and plenty of money.

**WEALTH.** This is a dream whose augury follows pretty closely the details of what is dreamed. One should not expect too quick a realization, but it seldom fails that a person dreaming of being rich fails to reach that enviable condition.

**WEAVING.** Seeing weavers at work, or weaving oneself is an omen of good news from an unexpected source.

**WEEPING.** To dream of weeping signifies that you will have unusual happiness.

**WELL.** Achievement of some strong desire is indicated by a dream of drawing water from a well.

**WHEAT.** A field of wheat is an omen of prosperity for yourself and your family.

**WILL.** A long life is presaged by a dream of making one's will.

**WINDMILL.** If the mill is in operation you will make a

small profit from your next business venture.

WINE. Happiness with your friends and family is predicted by a dream of drinking wine in moderation.

WOOL. A dream of wool, either on the sheep or in manufactured goods, foretells prosperity in business.

WREATH. Made with flowers or leaves a wreath is indicative of just what the colors signify. See COLOR.

## Y

YACHT. To dream of a yacht or other sailing boat used for pleasure predicts release from business or other cares.

YARN. If in your dreams you are knitting or darning with yarn, or holding yarn for someone to wind on a ball, you may confidently expect news of unexpected money.

YOLK. The yolk of a fresh egg seen or used in a dream, is a good augury for those engaged in manual labor of any kind.

YULETIDE. Christmas festivities in a dream are a lucky portent for those of a friendly disposition.

## Z

ZEBRA. An interesting and profitable experience is foretold by a dream of this unusual animal, seen either in its native state or in a zoological garden.

ZINC. Success in speculation and business is predicted by dreaming of zinc. It may be in sheet form or in the natural ore.

ZOOLOGICAL GARDEN. It is a sign of pleasurable travel in company with a distinguished person to dream of watching the animals in a zoo.

# STRANGE PROPHECIES, WARNINGS AND
## BAD LUCK

Perhaps your dream has nothing to do
good luck such as the making of money,
cheering news, or happiness within the family
prophesy a mystery that will be difficult or imp
solve; or an amusing situation that will have little m
or a new experience.

Some dreams are definite warnings against certain action
and if the warnings are heeded they may prove exceedingly
valuable. Others predict bad luck of one kind or another
that will be almost impossible to avoid. The last, of course,
should properly come under the head of warning dreams,
for, after all is said and done, we control our own destiny.

## STRANGE PORTENTS

### A

**ABANDONMENT.** To dream of being abandoned is a
portent of your failure to hold your own in your relations
with friends and business associates.

To abandon a family or someone who is in trouble
predicts some kind of grief.

To abandon a ship in a storm is a warning against
going on a sea voyage.

**ABDICATION.** If you dream that a monarch abdicates his
throne, it is a sign of war.

**ACCOUNTS.** Dreaming of having difficulty in keeping
accounts is a forerunner of harassing trials in business.

he, it
siness
anner

or any
o have

n in a
a tight
ourself.

yers who
g against
come.

ies deceit.

Beware of trusting                    acquaintances, and rely on tried and true friends.

ADDING. Business success is foretold by a dream of
adding up figures correctly, but if it seems impossible to
get the right total, the augury is one of disappointment.

ADULTERY. There are two aspects to a dream of
adultery: the actual committing of the act and the intent
to do so. Either is a forerunner of serious family
difficulties, but, strangely enough, the augury of a dream
of committing adultery is not as serious as that of a
dream of wishing to do so.

ADVENTURING. A dream of going out upon an adventure of one kind or another is a warning to go slowly in
making new investments.

ADVERTISING. It is a portent of a change in your
method of making a living to dream that you insert an

advertisement of any kind in a newspaper or other periodical.

**AGONY** (*See* Ache).

**AIRPLANE.** To dream of being a pilot of an airplane points toward achievement, either in business or in one of the arts.

If you are a passenger, it augurs immediate advancement in your affairs.

To fall with or from an airplane portends failure in one of your best laid plans.

**ALTAR.** This is a warning dream. If there is a priest officiating, you should avoid all worldly pleasures.

**AMMONIA.** You will be deceived by one of the people whom you considered friendly if you dream of smelling ammonia or using it for cleaning.

**AMPUTATION.** If you dream of having a leg or arm amputated, you should beware of taking any trip in either an automobile or railroad train for some time.

**ANKLE.** You will meet a fascinating person of the opposite sex if you dream of seeing an ankle that is pleasing in its proportions.

**ANTS.** Business will be good through your industry if you dream of ants, but if you kill any of them, the opposite may be expected.

**APES.** Trouble is in store for the person who dreams of these animals. It may portend sickness, so try to avoid colds.

**APPAREL.** Wearing fine clothes in a dream is a fortunate augury if the color is right. Look up COLOR (ch.V) for the significance of different hues.

**APRICOTS.** This fruit is a good sign if it is ripe, but if it is green, look out for family quarrels and business depression.

ARBOR. To walk through or sit in an arbor is a sign that someone will confide in you information that will be embarrassing unless you guard your tongue.

ARCH. It is not good luck to dream of passing under an arch. Your family will criticize your actions.

ARCHBISHOPS. If you dream of seeing an archbishop in his pontifical robes, your future life will probably be full of family troubles.

ARCHITECT. To see an architect at work is a sign that you will achieve some minor success. If you dream of being an architect, it means that you will make a change in your business.

ARM. Divorce either in your immediate family or in that of someone close to you is foretold by a dream of having an arm amputated.

To dream of having your arm around a stranger of the opposite sex predicts an experience of which you will be ashamed.

ARREST. If you dream of being arrested by a policeman, you will be likely to have an increase in your income.

ARTIST. Dreaming of seeing an artist at work is a warning to keep on with your present situation.

To dream of posing in the nude for an artist is a sign that your frankness will win a high position for you.

ASPARAGUS. The odor of asparagus is a portent that you will meet someone of the opposite sex who will reveal his or her innermost secrets.

ASS. This animal is a symbol of stupidity, and a dream about it is a warning to be careful to investigate thoroughly any proposition that may be made to you.

**ATHLETE.** It is not fortunate to dream of an athlete engaged in contests such as racing, pole-vaulting, putting the shot, or wrestling. It predicts a struggle in which you will not be likely to win.

**ATTIC.** To dream of being in an attic predicts a period of discontentment which is likely to end in a satisfactory adjustment of your difficulties.

**ATTORNEY** (*See* Lawyer).

**AUNT.** You will be criticized for something you have done whether you deserve it or not.

**AVALANCHE.** This may be either a good or bad dream. It is propitious except when you dream of being smothered by it. Then you may expect a period of financial instability.

**AXE.** This is a warning to go slow with any action that you have made up your mind to take.
    A dream of chopping wood with an axe predicts a new and interesting but not too reliable acquaintance.

## B

**BABY.** For a woman, married or single, to dream of having a baby is a sign that a pet ambition will be realized.
    For a man to have this dream (which is not unusual) the portent is not so good. He is likely to be involved in a scandal that will have serious consequences.
    A dream of seeing happy and smiling babies augurs contentment within the family circle.

**BACHELOR.** For a married man or woman to dream of being single again is a warning against the temptations that come with "the dangerous age."

**BACK.** Don't lend money to anyone if you dream of seeing a nude back. The warning is even stronger if the back is of the opposite sex.

To slap a back in a dream is a portent of loss of money.

BACKGAMMON. There will be an unwelcome visitor at your house if you dream of playing backgammon.

BAG. Opening a bag in a dream is a presage of a surprising experience that may have a lasting effect on your career.

BAKING. Illness is foretold by a dream of baking bread or cake.

BALDNESS. This dream is a forerunner of hard luck both in family life and in business.

BALL. To dream of being at a ball in the company of well-dressed and gay dancers is a portent of an elevation to a much higher position in social life.

BANK. It is a sign of financial difficulties to dream of transacting business in a bank.

BAPTISM. The rite of baptism, either by sprinkling or total immerision, is a portent of your trying an experiment that will cause you considerable trouble before it succeeds.

BARROOM. If you dream of becoming inebriated in a barroom, you may expect disquieting news from an old friend.

BASEBALL. Those who drive motor cars should regard a dream of this game as a warning to exercise caution, as it is an unlucky sign for those who travel.

BATHING. The significance of this dream depends on several factors. If you are taking a cold bath, the prediction is that you will meet with an unexpected rebuff or disappointment.

To dream of taking a warm bath means a new opportunity that will work out favorably for you.

A woman who dreams of taking a milk bath should be warned against careless association with men of whose intentions she does not feel sure.

Turkish baths signify that someone will apologize to you.

BATS. Death is predicted by a dream of seeing bats. At best, the dreamer will have a loathsome experience.

BAYONET. Someone with whom you have had a quarrel will turn out to be a good friend if you dream of using a bayonet.

To dream of being stabbed by a bayonet means that you will be cheated in a business deal.

BEANS. A dream of eating beans augurs disgrace, or, at the very least, great embarrassment which will be difficult to live down.

BEAR. If in a dream a bear chases you, it is a sign that you will lose money through inattention to business.

BEARD. Long beards seen in a dream predict a succession of irritating business difficulties.

If you dream of combing your own beard and it is full of snarls, you will be likely to quarrel with your relatives.

Having your beard trimmed is a portent of a slight improvement in business.

BED. To dream of going to bed with a stranger of the opposite sex is a warning against making new acquaintances too easily.

BEER. Drinking beer in a dream, if alone or in pleasant company, is a forerunner of activity in new lines of endeavor.

BEETLES. It bodes no good to dream of beetles. Hard luck may come in any number of ways, so it is necessary for the dreamer to be especially careful, especially in matters pertaining to trade.

**BEGGAR.** It is a sign of an improvement in your financial and family affairs if you dream of giving alms to a beggar.

**BELLOWS.** You will have a struggle against adversity if you dream of blowing a fire with bellows.

**BELLY.** If you dream of looking at your own belly, it portends a pleasant attitude toward your condition of life.

If you gaze at another's belly, either a man's or a woman's, it is an omen of an achievement that will not be creditable but will bring you money.

**BENCH.** Don't trust too much in promises if you dream of sitting on a bench.

**BETTING.** This dream is a warning against making wagers, whether you win or not.

**BIGAMY.** It is not auspicious to dream that you have taken two or more mates. It predicts illness of a serious nature.

**BILLIARDS.** To dream of playing billiards foretells the finding of an old letter that will cause you trouble.

Watching a game of billards denotes that something will be revealed that you would prefer to have kept secret.

**BIRTH.** It is a warning against loose friendships for a maiden to dream of giving birth to a child.

**BISCUITS.** Trouble is foretold by a dream of eating biscuits. It may mean either quarrels or illness.

**BISHOPS.** Worries over marital difficulties are presaged by a dream of seeing a bishop in his clerical robes.

**BITE.** If someone bites you in a dream, even playfully, it is an omen of a loss that may come through a lawsuit.

**BLACKBERRIES.** Like everything black, this fruit predicts harm, either through illness or accident.

**BLEEDING.** Illness or death are foretold by a dream of bleeding in any manner.

**BLINDFOLD.** You are in danger of a serious accident if you dream of wearing a blindfold. The omen is worse if you stumble in the dream.

**BLOTTING PAPER.** Be warned against revealing any of your secrets to anybody, if you dream of using blotting paper.

**BOAT.** If the weather is stormy and the water rough, it predicts a change for the worse in the fortunes of the dreamer.

To fall overboard from a boat is an indication that you will fail in your next business venture.

**BONES.** A dream of seeing piles of bones is a presage of unhappiness through illness.

If you see a very thin person whose bones appear to stick out, be warned of impending disaster.

**BOOKS.** It is an omen of minor honors that will be conferred on you if you dream of seeing or reading books.

**BOSOM.** An ample bosom on a woman is a presage of increasing responsibilities that will bring worthwhile reward.

**BOWLING.** You may look forward to success in business if you dream of bowling, particularly if you make a strike.

**BRAMBLES.** Be cautious in any business deal that you may have in prospect after dreaming of getting into brambles.

**BRANDY.** Sipping brandy in a dream is a warning against false friends.

**BREAKING.** To break anything in a dream portends grief from the loss of a friend, by death or otherwise.

**BREASTS.** If of the opposite sex, breasts signify gain, but it may be financial or spiritual.

**BREATH.** Failure is indicated by a dream of being out of breath for whatever cause.

**BRIDGE.** To dream of losing at the game of bridge is an indication that your friends will turn from you when you need them most. Winning at bridge portends gay pleasures.

**BRISTLES** (*See* Toothbrush).

**BROOM.** Careful attention to your business will be rewarded if you dream of sweeping with a broom.

**BROTHEL.** Dreaming of being in a brothel foretells that there is some easy money in prospect for you, but the dream carries a warning against engaging in any business that is not strictly ethical.

**BRUSHING.** It is a sign of an increased income if you dream of brushing your clothes. A whisk broom is the most auspicious.

**BUGLE.** The sound of a bugle heard in a dream is an omen of coming misfortune.

**BURDEN.** Any kind of a burden carried in a dream predicts trials and worries of a personal nature.

**BURGLAR.** If you dream of encountering a burglar, you should guard your actions carefully in connection with plans for buying property.

**BUTTERMILK.** Drinking this beverage in a dream is a forerunner of a great disappointment.

**BUYING.** It is not propitious to dream of purchasing articles. It presages failure in business.

## C

**CABBAGE.** A field of cabbage seen in a dream is a portent of the acquisition of property that will give you trouble.

To eat cabbage in a dream predicts trouble with your relatives. To cook it is an augury of trouble with your teeth.

The odor of boiling cabbage is a forerunner of illness.

**CABIN.** In the woods, a cabin is an omen of contentment, but to dream of being in a ship's cabin portends trouble on account of enemies.

**CALOMEL.** If you dream of taking calomel, you will take a short trip.

To dream of giving it to someone else is a warning against running unnecessary risks.

**CALVES.** The animals are omens of a business opportunity that may add considerably to your income.

Women's calves seen in a dream are a warning to be discreet in your relations with the opposite sex.

**CAMEL.** An unusual adventure is in store for you if you dream of seeing one or more camels.

**CAMERA.** To use a camera in a dream is usually a sign of disappointment, especially in connection with one you believed to be a friend.

**CANAL.** Stagnant water in a canal is an omen of discontent in family life.

**CANDY.** It is prophetic of a lucky turn of some kind if you dream of making candy.

**CARDS** (*See* Playing Cards).

**CARS** (*See also* Motor Cars). Street cars, either seen or ridden on, are an omen of petty annoyances that will come largely from your own fault.

To dream of going to bed in a sleeping-car is an augury of achievement after much difficulty.

Freight cars denote an increase in your possessions without any satisfaction therefrom.

Riding in an ordinary car on a railroad train presages a trip that will fail to bring you pleasure.

**CARTRIDGE.** It is very unlucky to dream of putting a cartridge into a gun or pistol. It is a forerunner of an accusation that will be made against you.

**CASH.** To dream of handling cash is a sign that you will handle very little of your own.

**CASTOR OIL.** If you dream of taking castor oil, you will do well to heed the advice of someone who is trying to help you.

**CATARACT.** This is a luck omen if in your dream there is a sense of pleasure. If the cataract frightens you, the portent is ominous.

**CAVE.** You will be forgotten by someone you care for if you dream of entering a cave.

**CELLAR.** A cold or a damp cellar is a portent of bad news from a relative who lives at a distance.

If you dream of being locked in a cellar, it is a presage of illness.

**CEMETERY.** A strange experience in which machinery will have an important part is predicted by dreaming of picking blackberries in an old and deserted cemetery.

**CHAIR.** To dream of someone sitting in a rocking chair foretells the arrival of a disagreeable visitor.

**CHALK.** You will be likely to lose considerable money if you dream of writing on a blackboard or slate with chalk.

**CHASE.** If an enemy chases you in a dream, and you get away, it is a sign that you will see an improvement in your business.
    If the enemy catches you, the portent is one of failure.

**CHEATING.** It is better to dream of being cheated than to cheat. Both dreams, however, point to family difficulties.

**CHEERING.** To hear cheering in a dream is an omen of shame for some unworthy action.

**CHEMISE.** A man or woman who dreams of this garment, either on someone or not, should regard it as a warning against light relations with anyone of the opposite sex.

**CHILBLAINS.** A dream of chilblains on the feet predicts an argument with someone whom you like. If the chilblains are on the hands, it means that you will meet an interesting stranger.

**CHILDREN.** The significance of this dream depends on the state of the children. If they are well and happy, the portent could not be better. Otherwise, the dream is an omen of sickness.

**CHRISTENING.** This ought to be a fortunate omen, but it foretells a succession of petty troubles.

**CHURCH.** It is bad luck to dream of being in a church, whether or not there is a service in progress. It is a sign that you will encounter some distressing times.

**CIGAR.** For a man, or woman, to dream of smoking a cigar is an augury of comfort in old age.

CIGARETTE. Smoking a cigarette in a dream portends a period of wholesome recreation.

CINDER. In your eye, a cinder is a portent of happenings that will be disagreeable but, if met with fortitude, will not last long.

CLARET. Like any red wine, claret in a dream is a symbol of good fortune. Look up *red* COLOR (ch. V).

CLERGYMEN (*See* Bishops, Pulpit). Criticism from your in-laws will follow a dream of clergymen seen inside a church.

CLOTHES. Dreaming that your clothes are soiled is an augury of meeting someone of loose morals.

CLOUDS. Black, threatening clouds foretell a new disturbing influence in your life.
   To dream of seeing clouds at night is a forerunner of unpleasant discovery about one of your friends.

COCKTAILS. If you dream of drinking cocktails with one of the opposite sex, you will have cause to worry for fear some early indiscretion will be discovered.

COFFIN. A dead person seen in a coffin is a dream that presages an accident. If the person in the coffin seems to be alive, it is a portent that you will be slandered.

COLD. It is a warning to guard your conduct if you dream of having a cold.

COLLISION (*See* Cars). To dream of being in a vehicle that collides with another vehicle foretells injury to one of the limbs. This applies equally to horse-drawn or motor propelled vehicles, and includes boats of any kind.

COMET. Short-lived pleasures are predicted by a dream of a comet streaking across the sky.

**COMMITTEE.** If in your dream you are appointed to a committee, you are likely to be the victim of a base accusation.

**CONCUBINE** (*See* Harlot).

**CONFETTI.** To dream of being sprinkled by confetti is an augury of minor irritations that will affect your disposition if you let them.

**CONGRATULATIONS.** Received in a dream, congratulations point toward an occurrence that will require condolences.

**CORKSCREW.** Using a corkscrew in a dream predicts that you will be cheated in a business deal.

**CORPSE** (*See* Coffin). Unhappiness is foretold by a dream of seeing a dead person lying out in the open. Bad news may be expected.
   The corpse of an animal betokens a small financial loss.
   An ancient corpse, such as an Egyptian mummy, is an omen of the raking up of an old wrong.

**CORSET.** Women who dream of putting on a corset may look forward to being deceived by an acquaintance of long standing.
   If a man dreams of putting on a woman's corset, he will suffer ridicule to his great embarrassment.

**COWSLIP.** A pleasant experience with friends is in store for you if you dream of these flowers.

**CRADLE.** It is bad luck for an unmarried person to dream of rocking a baby in a cradle. For those who are married, the omen is propitious. It signifies a happy future.

**CRIPPLE.** It is a sign that you will meet an interesting

person of another race if you dream of helping a cripple in any way.

CROSSROADS. You will be puzzled about some business deal if you dream of arriving at a crossroads, but you will make a satisfactory decision.

CUPBOARD. An empty cupboard seen in a dream portends diminishing financial resources.

CURTAINS. Soiled white curtains are a forerunner of good luck to those engaged in literary or other artistic work.

CUSPIDOR. Failure to succeed in a pet project is predicted if you try to spit into a cuspidor and miss. Any dream of using a cuspidor foretells disappointment.

CUT. A dream of cutting your finger means that you will not receive money that you have confidently expected.

CYMBALS. To hear or see the clash of cymbals in a dream augurs a great change in your mode of living, usually for the better but sometimes for the worse.

## D

DAGGER. A dagger dream portends a threat to your local reputation. It is a warning against any act that may be wrongly interpreted.

DAISIES. Blooming in a field, daisies portend simple but real joys. In a vase, out of season, they point toward sadness.

DANDELIONS. A dream of these flowers is a forerunner of some kind of embarrassing experience. Worn in a buttonhole, they are a sign that you will be ridiculed.

DEAD (*See* Coffin, Corpse).

**DEBT.** A dream of being in debt is a portent of harassing business worries.

**DEED.** Signing a deed in a dream prophesies a legal action that will probably be decided against you.

**DENTIST.** If you dream of having dental work done, you may expect a letter that will give you cause for worry.

If the dream includes having a tooth drawn, the omen is of a loss of money.

**DESK.** Working at a desk in a dream presages irritating family concerns.

**DESSERT.** To dream of eating a rich dessert indicates that you will enjoy some luxury that formerly you have had to go without.

**DETECTIVE.** You will be placed in an embarrassing situation that may turn out to be serious if you dream of being a detective.

If you dream of being arrested by a detective, you are in danger from your enemies.

**DICTIONARY.** Quarrels are predicted by a dream of looking up words in this reference book.

**DIGGING.** It is an omen of hard work that is likely to reward you handsomely if you dream of digging with a spade.

**DISEASE.** Contagious or loathsome diseases in a dream presage unhappiness that can be avoided by the use of good judgment.

**DISGUISE.** You are warned to be perfectly frank in your business affairs if you dream of wearing a disguise that hides your real identity.

**DOMINOES.** Playing at dominoes in a dream presages the

visit to your home of a person you do not like, but to whom you must be pleasant.

DRUMS. The muffled beat of drums dimly heard in a dream is a portent of tragic happenings to someone of whom you are fond.

DRUNKENNESS. Seeing other people under the influence of liquor is a forerunner of accident through carelessness.
    To dream of being drunk is a distinct warning against taking chances in investing your money.

DUMMY. Dreaming of a dummy is an omen of your failure to succeed in an enterprise where ordinarily good judgment would help you out.

DUEL. An accident is predicted by a dream of fighting a duel.

DWARF. Problems that appear to have no solution will be solved for you if you dream of a dwarf or midget. This applies as well to animals and plants.

DYEING. It is a sign of coming business success to dream of dyeing your hair.

DYING. To dream of dying predicts illness or accident.
    To dream of seeing someone else die is an augury of difficult times through family misunderstandings.

E

EARTHQUAKE. This is a warning dream. It may foretell war or some other great disturbance, or it may be a forerunner of some mental shock.

EATING. It is an unfortunate augury to dream of eating alone.

ECHO. A strange experience with someone of the opposite sex is predicted by a dream of hearing an echo.

**ECLIPSE.** Whether of the sun or moon, this dream is a portent of dread and unhappiness.

**ELECTION.** If in a dream you are running for election to some local or national position, it prophesies failure in business.

**ELEVATOR.** To be stuck in an elevator between floors is an indication that you should guard your conduct.

To be in a falling elevator is a premonition of financial loss.

Riding in an elevator is propitious if the car is going up; otherwise if it is going down.

To dream of operating an elevator is a sign that you will make money.

**EMERALD.** Someone of whom you are very fond will move to a distant city if you dream of an emerald.

**ENEMY.** It is an omen of good fortune to dream of your enemy.

**ENGINE** (*See* Machinery).

**EPIDEMIC.** Many mental difficulties are presaged by a dream of being in an epidemic.

**ESCAPE.** A dream of an escape from a dangerous situation is a sign that there are forces at work that may result in getting you into trouble.

**EXCUSES.** It foretells that you will be in a position where you will have to explain your actions if you dream of making excuses.

**EXECUTION.** Sickness is prophesied by a dream of seeing a man or woman executed for murder or other crime.

FACTORY. A factory in operation portends great activity in business with an excellent chance of making money. To dream of working in a factory is an omen that faithfulness in your chosen work will be rewarded.

FAINTING. A warning is contained in a dream of fainting. It means that you are careless in your choice of companions and your methods of recreation.

FALLING. This dream is merely a warning to "watch your step" in connection with business, members of the opposite sex, and physical fitness.

FALSEHOOD. If you dream of being caught in telling a falsehood, you will be likely to suffer an injury of some kind. If the dream is of detecting someone else in a falsehood, the augury is propitious.

FATHER. To dream of one's father portends a complete change in living conditions. A city dweller is likely to change to the country, and a resident of a rural section will move to the city.

FATIGUE. Unpleasant developments in your social life are predicted by a dream of being tired.

FEAST. A dream of feasting is auspicious except where there are indications of gluttony, drunkenness or other bad manners.

FEET. Loss of standing in your community is foretold if you dream of looking at your own feet; at another's feet—loss of money.

FEVER. To dream of having a fever is a portent of happenings that will be worrisome but not serious.

FINGERNAILS. Dirty fingernails, either your own or someone else's, seen in a dream are an indication that you will be charged with a crime.

Clean and well-kept fingernails, with a high polish are an omen of deceitful acquaintances whom you see frequently.

FIRE ENGINE. Curious occupations, which may bring you in contact with interesting but unscrupulous people, are predicted by dreaming of a fire engine on its way to a fire.

FISH NET. It betokens a surprise of some kind, either pleasant or unpleasant, if you dream of mending a fish net.

FITS. If you dream of having fits, you will be harrassed by bill collectors. To see another person having a fit is an omen of losing some prized possession.

FLAG. A woman who dreams of a waving flag is likely to find that some man whom she believed to be indifferent is very much interested in her.

FLEAS. To dream of being bitten by fleas is a presage of suffering from evil reports circulated by your enemies.

FLEET. Seeing a fleet of battleships is an omen of upset business conditions.

A fleet of fishing schooners predicts a tragic happening to one of your friends.

FLIES. Disease is foretold by a dream of house flies, especially if they are around food in the dining-room or kitchen.

FLOATING. You will be puzzled by the behavior of your friends if you dream of floating.

FLOWERS. In general it is lucky to dream of flowers, but if the odor is unpleasant, it is not a fortunate augury. Look up COLORS (ch. V).

**FOLIAGE.** Green leaves are prophecies of well-being. If the foliage is dead, the omen is one of unhappiness.

**FOOD.** Plenty of food in a dream foretells business success.

    Too little food is a forerunner of distress.

    Too much food is an omen of sensual pleasures.

**FOOTBALL.** If you dream of attending a football game, you are likely to find profit in a new undertaking.

**FORGERY.** To dream that your name has been forged on a check or other document is a warning against being too trustful of your business associates.

**FORT.** It is bad luck to dream of seeing or being inside a fort.

**FRAUD.** Beware of your conduct in business if you dream of defrauding anyone. If the dream is of being defrauded the omen is a good one.

**FROGS.** Watch every penny carefully if you dream of hearing frogs.

**FROST.** Seen on a window, frost betokens an unusual occurrence in your social life.

**FUNERAL.** A long period of distress, either financial or otherwise, may be expected after dreaming of seeing or attending a funeral.

**FURNITURE.** It is a sign of failure to accomplish your ambition if you dream of stumbling over furniture, especially in a dark room.

    To dream of rearranging furniture is a sign of insanity, though not necessarily your own.

    Re-upholstering furniture in a dream predicts some small but pleasant achievement.

# G

**GAG.** If you dream of having a gag put in your mouth, you will find that you have many obstacles to overcome in business and family life.

**GAITERS.** Social triumphs are predicted by dreaming of wearing gaiters.

**GALLOWS.** You will be frustrated in your immediate plans for bettering yourself if you see a gallows in your dream.
Sudden and unexpected bad luck is predicted by a dream of being led to the gallows.

**GAMBLING.** There is every chance of loss if you dream of winning at the races or at games of chance.
The augury is better if you dream of losing.

**GAME.** To dream of eating game is an omen of meeting a prominent person under unusual circumstances.

**GAS.** Illuminating gas in any form, seen or smelled, foretells difficulties with the police authorities.

**GHOST.** This is a dream that predicts an experience of a humorous nature that will probably work out to your profit.

**GIN.** Your judgment in an important matter will be severely criticized if you dream of drinking gin, either straight or mixed with other ingredients.

**GOD.** You will probably meet people whose hypocrisy will disgust you if you dream of seeing God.
If you dream of praying to God, the omen is toward contentment with what you have.
To dream of hearing God speak is an augury of happiness through friendship.

**GOLD MINE.** It signifies disappointment if you dream of working in a gold mine. The portent is less unfortunate if you dream of finding gold.

**GOLDFISH.** Seen in a bowl of water, goldfish predict embarrassment through a surprise meeting. In an outdoor pool they foretell a slight injury.

**GOLF.** To dream of playing golf indicates that your business affairs need close attention to save them from going to ruin.

**GONG.** The ringing of a gong, unless it has a very musical note, denotes an unpleasant surprise. If the note is musical it foretells an unexpected visit from a relative.

**GOOSE.** A roasted goose seen or eaten in a dream is an indication that you should guard against careless association with strangers.

**GRAPES.** You are likely to be entertained lavishly by a very rich person if you dream of eating grapes. If you eat them from the vine, it also predicts an inheritance.

**GRASSHOPPERS.** Dreaming of one or more grasshoppers usually precedes business reverses of a serious nature.

**GRAVE.** This dream is always a prediction of misfortune. It signifies loss, whether from death or other causes, and at best it is a warning to avoid even the appearance of evil.

A dream of digging a grave is a prediction that a close friend will leave you.

**GRAVY.** Your reputation for honesty and morality will be in danger if you dream of eating gravy. If you spill it on your clothes, you will suffer a wrong from an inferior.

**GREYHOUND.** To dream of a greyhound is to be in danger on account of the kind of company you keep.

**GROCERIES.** If you dream of a store of groceries on your shelves, the augury is one of prosperity.

**GULLS.** Swooping overhead, gulls are a portent of your being exposed for some wrong you did years ago.

**GUNS.** Shots from guns, either big or little, foretell sudden changes in your financial condition, for better or for worse.

Seeing big guns in a fort or on a battleship is a sign that you will meet a person of importance.

# H

**HAIRPIN.** For a man to dream of having a hairpin denotes a discovery that will bring him money.

**HAMMER.** Using a hammer in a dream predicts physical pain.

**HAMMOCK.** Sitting in a hammock with one of the opposite sex is a warning against indiscreet conduct.

Sleeping in a hammock is a prediction of travel in foreign countries over a long period.

**HANDCUFFS.** You will be likely to find yourself restrained by circumstances you cannot control if you dream of wearing handcuffs.

**HANGING.** This dream bodes ill, but it is better to dream of being hanged than to be a spectator at a hanging.

**HAT.** To dream of wearing a hat that does not fit you signifies that your pride will cause you trouble.

To lose a hat predicts a shameful experience.

**HATCHET.** A small hatchet used in a dream predicts that you will do someone a wrong if you do not curb any tendency you may have toward gossip.

**HATE.** This is a dream of warning against giving way to hate for anyone.

**HAWK.** You are in danger of being cheated by someone you know well if you dream of this bird of prey.

To kill a hawk is a warning to avoid giving cause for criticism in your business dealings.

**HEARSE.** A dream of a hearse is an omen of a serious but not necessarily fatal illness.

**HEAVEN** (*See* God).

**HEATHER.** Growing heather seen in a dream is a good sign for actors, singers, artists, writers, and others engaged in similar pursuits.

**HEIR.** It signifies the opposite if you dream of falling heir to a legacy.

If you dream of making someone your heir, it foretells sickness.

**HERMIT.** Seeing a hermit in your dream foretells a period of great loneliness.

To dream of taking up the life of a hermit is an omen of doing something that will make you unpopular.

**HERO.** If you dream of doing a heroic deed, you will be likely to get into a quarrel with your wife or husband.

**HIDING.** It is an omen of serious difficulties with your employer if you dream of hiding from someone.

**HIVE.** Sharp pain of short duration is predicted by a dream of seeing or working with beehives.

**HIVES.** Some harassing nervous experience will be yours if you dream of having this skin eruption.

**HOLLY.** A dream of this Christmas plant foretells good

fortune and ease, but with many small irritations.

HONEYSUCKLE. To see or smell this lovely flower in a dream augurs relief from mental or financial pressure.

HOOP-SKIRT. You are warned against committing an immodest act if you dream of a woman wearing a hoop-skirt.

HORNS. If you dream of seeing a man or woman with horns, or that you have them yourself, it is a sign that you are headed for trouble through bad judgment in choosing companions.

HOSPITAL. Beware of schemes of the opposite sex if you dream of being in a hospital, either as a patient or visitor.
    If you dream of being a nurse or doctor, you may look forward to happiness.

HOTHOUSE. You will travel in a warm country if you dream of being in a hothouse.

HURDLE. Meeting a hurdle in your dream and failing to leap over it prophesies loss or disappointment.
    The augury is excellent if you get over the hurdle.

HURRICANE. Dreaming of being in a hurricane on land or sea is a presage of struggle against adversity.

HYPOCRISY. You should be on your guard against deceitful acquaintances if you dream of hypocrisy on the part of your associates.

# I

IDOL. It is a sign that you are about to make a great mistake if you dream of idols, so this may be regarded as a warning to "watch your step."

INCEST. This is a dream that predicts serious illness from overindulgence.

**INDIGESTION.** To dream of suffering from indigestion is a sign that you will be pursued by your creditors.

**INFANT.** A healthy and attractive infant augurs success, but a sickly baby predicts failure.

**INJURY.** This dream foretells a series of minor accidents that will be more irritating than serious.

**INK.** The color of the ink used in a dream governs the prediction. Look up COLORS (ch. V).

**INSECTS.** To dream of being annoyed by insects is a prophecy of trouble with your relatives.

**INTESTINES.** You are likely to be bothered by a matter that weighs on your conscience if you dream of seeing the intestines of either humans or animals.

**INVALID.** A dream of seeing or being an invalid is a warning against carelessness as to your physical welfare.
   If you dream of nursing an invalid, you are likely to have trouble with your teeth.

**IRON.** This is an unfortunate dream, as the color is black.

**ITCH.** The chances are that you will be harassed by many petty annoyances if you dream of itching.

**J**

**JAM.** Embarrassment through no fault of your own is prophesied by a dream of eating jam or jelly.
   It is a sign of a surprise of some sort if you dream of seeing a child eating it.

**JELLY** (*See* Jam).

**JEWELRY.** It presages criticism of a virulent nature if you dream of wearing unusual or bizarre jewelry.

**JOLLITY.** A change of fortune is predicted by a dream of being in jolly company.

**JUDGE.** If you dream of appearing before a judge, whether in a court of law or elsewhere, you will be likely to experience difficulty with relatives.

**JUNE.** It is an augury of the successful accomplishment of an experiment if in your dream you think of this month.

**JURY.** To dream of sitting on a jury is a forerunner of dissatisfaction with your family affairs.

## K

**KANGAROO.** For a married woman to dream of a kangaroo is an omen of a miscarriage. For a man, it indicates terror from an unknown cause.

**KEEPSAKE.** If in a dream someone gives you a keepsake it signifies that you will have to accept new responsibility.

**KEG.** Drawing beer or wine from a keg is an omen of convivial times in store for you.

**KEYHOLE.** Shame is foretold by a dream of trying to look through a keyhole.
    Failure in business concerns is likely to follow a dream of having difficulty in getting a key into a keyhole.

**KITTEN.** If you are scratched by a kitten in a dream, you will come in contact with an exceedingly disagreeable person.

**KNITTING.** A man or woman who dreams of knitting will need the services of a doctor before many days.

**KNOCKING.** To hear knocking, rapping or pounding in a dream is a warning against the evil tongues of people who are seeking your downfall.

# L

**LABEL.** A label seen or placed on a bottle, package or trunk is an augury of unusual business activity. If you have trouble in deciphering the label, you will have a surprise.

**LADDER.** To dream of having difficulty in adjusting a ladder against a house indicates marital upsets.

If in a dream you walk under a ladder, you will be likely to have a slight accident.

Seeing a ladder in use by a fireman is an omen of business success.

**LAMENTATION.** Loss of money or a friend is foretold by a dream of seeing and hearing a person lamenting a tragedy.

**LAMP.** Any kind of a lamp is a sign of the solution of a problem that has puzzled you.

**LARD.** A trusted acquaintance is likely to deceive you if you dream of cooking with lard.

**LAUNDRY.** Soiled laundry seen in a dream points to an accusation of carelessness that will be made against you.

**LAWSUIT.** It is a sign of deterioration in business affairs if you dream of suing or being sued.

**LAWYER.** To dream of meeting a lawyer socially is a portent of being involved in a scandal.

**LEAKING.** You will be likely to have financial losses if you dream of a leaking faucet or of any container for liquids.

**LEATHER.** The smell of leather in a dream presages a meeting with a foreigner from a remote land.

**LEAVINGS.** The leavings on plates after a meal are an

omen of ill luck in connection with any building enterprise.

LEECHES. You are likely to be cheated in a business deal if you dream of seeing leeches or having them applied to your body.

LEOPARD. A dream of being attacked by a leopard presages an accident.

Seeing this wild animal in captivity indicates that you will be able to overcome a serious obstacle.

LETTUCE. You must guard against showing your dislike for an influential person if you dream of lettuce in any form.

LICE. If you dream of this vermin, you will have to apologize to someone who is beneath you.

LIGHT (*See also* Lamp). A very bright light, seen in a dream signifies new knowledge that will be of monetary value if you make the best use of it.

LIMES. A strange experience with a person you do not know well is predicted by drinking the juice of this fruit.

Picking limes is a sign that you will discover an old letter that will cause you concern.

LIQUOR. If you dream of giving liquor to a child, the omen is of a very serious illness in your family.

LIQUEUR. It will be necessary to be on your guard against those who flatter you if you dream of drinking liqueurs or cordials.

LOUSE (*See* Lice).

LUMBER. Great business activity may be expected after dreaming of lumber in piles.

**LUXURY.** This portends success in business only if it appears that the luxury has been earned through honest endeavor. Otherwise it foretells misfortune.

**LYING.** A dream of telling a lie is an ill omen. It is a warning of loss of friends and of standing in your community.

## M

**MACARONI.** There will be a strong likelihood that you will suffer reverses, probably slight ones, if you dream of eating macaroni.

A dream of cooking macaroni portends that you will be the victim of fraud.

**MAGICIAN.** It is a sign of a pleasant surprise to dream of seeing a magician doing mystifying tricks.

**MAGISTRATE** (*See* Judge).

**MANACLES.** Unfortunate happenings are in store for you if you dream of being manacled.

To dream of putting manacles on another is a warning against loose company.

**MANURE.** Cleaning manure out of stables is a sign of a new opportunity.

**MAP.** It is an augury of wandering in foreign countries to dream of tracing a route on a map or on a globe of the world.

**MARKET.** To dream of buying food in a market is a presage of a new idea that will be profitable to you.

**MARSH.** Walking through a marsh in a dream denotes that you will meet many obstacles and dangers in your business and social life.

**MASQUERADE.** You should beware of associations with

deceitful persons if you dream of attending a masquerade party in costume.

MAT. It predicts bad luck to dream of tripping over a mat. Wiping one's feet on a mat is an omen of scandalous accusations.

MAUSOLEUM. You are likely to hear of the death of an acquaintance of long standing if you dream of seeing a mausoleum.

MEASLES. This disease augurs a long siege of arguments with your in-laws, with a satisfactory termination.

MEAT. A dream of eating meat that is well cooked and of good flavor is a good omen, but if the meat is raw or tainted, it predicts illness of a serious nature.

MEDICINE. Someone is likely to act in an offensive manner toward you if you dream of taking medicine.
To dream of giving medicine is a prediction that one of your ambitions will be thwarted.

MICE. Petty irritations will be yours if you dream of seeing or catching mice in a trap.

MILK. To drink milk in a dream and find that it is sour is an omen of disappointment.

MINISTER (*See* Bishops, Pulpit, Clergymen).

MOLASSES. It is an augury of failure in an enterprise close to your heart if you dream of eating molasses.
Selling molasses is an augury of profit in your business.

MORGUE. Bad luck in any one of several different ways may be expected after a dream of visiting a morgue.
If you dream of identifying one of the corpses, you are likely to hear of disquieting news by mail or telegraph.

**MOTHER-IN-LAW.** It is seldom that a mother-in-law dream is not a forerunner of family misunderstandings. The dream is a warning against losing your temper.

**MOTOR CAR** (*See* Cars).

**MOTOR TRUCK** (*See* Collision).

**MOUSE** (*See* Mice).

**MUD.** Someone will seek to blacken your reputation if you dream of being splashed with mud.

To dream of getting your feet muddy is a warning against indiscretions with the opposite sex.

**MURDER.** To commit murder in a dream is a sign of business profit in a manner of which you may have reason to be ashamed.

**MUSEUM.** It is a sign of rapidly changing conditions in your business conditions if you dream of examining art treasures in an art museum.

# N

**NAGGING.** One may expect trials resulting from misunderstandings with relatives if he or she dreams of being nagged.

**NEIGHBOR.** It is a sign of new social contacts if you dream of meeting a neighbor in the vicinity of your home.

**NETTLES.** Being stung by nettles in a dream augurs the receipt of news that you can use with profit.

**NEWSPAPER.** Dreaming of working for a newspaper indicates that you will have a troublous but interesting career.

Someone will be a nuisance to you if you dream of reading a newspaper.

**NIGHTCAP.** There is amusement in store for you after a dream of wearing a nightcap to bed.

**NOISE.** Hearing a loud noise in a dream presages a surprise that may lead to an improvement in your financial condition.

**NOSE.** If someone's nose is the most important part of a dream, you will suffer from the curiosity of your neighbors. You are warned against indiscreet conduct.

**NUTMEGS.** These are a prophecy of someone trying to cheat you in a business deal.

## O

**OASIS.** It is an augury of the beginning of a new enterprise, which has every chance of success, to dream of reaching an oasis after a trip across the desert.

**OBITUARY.** To dream of reading the obituary of a friend or acquaintance predicts the loss of money.
　　If you dream of reading your own obituary, you will receive important news.

**OCULIST.** Dreaming of having your eyes examined by an oculist is a portent of having to decide an important question in which your best judgment will be required.

**OLIVES.** Eating unripe olives in a dream is a forerunner of shame.

**OMELET.** To make or eat an omelet in a dream prophesies that you are in danger of doing something for which you will be sorry.

**OPAL.** If you are given an opal, or if you wear one in a dream, you will be misunderstood through no fault of your own.

OPERA (*See* Melody, Music, Orchestra, ch. V).

OPERATION. Having an operation in a dream is a sign that radical treatment of your business problems will bring ultimate success.

OPIUM. You are likely to get into shameful difficulties with a member of the opposite sex if you dream of smoking opium.

OPTICIAN. If you dream of getting glasses from an optician, the augury is of a sea trip in the company of someone whom you do not know.

ORGAN (*See* Melody, Music, Orchestra, ch. V).

ORPHAN ASYLUM. It is an omen of opportunities for doing good both to yourself and others if you dream of visiting an orphan asylum.

OSTRICH. A man should be very careful to avoid entangling alliances with women if he dreams of seeing ostriches. This is also a warning dream for women.

OUTBOARD MOTOR. A series of surprising and generally happy events is predicted by a dream of using an outboard motor.

OWL. Enemies are plotting to place you in an embarrassing position if you dream of seeing or hearing an owl.

P

PACK. To dream of seeing a man or woman bearing a pack on his or her back presages a serious illness.

PADLOCK. The frustration of some pet ambition is predicted by a dream of finding a door padlocked. If you succeed in unlocking it, the augury is a good one.

PAIL. Carrying a pail in a dream is a sign of a quarrel with someone of whom you are very fond. If the pail is full of liquid which slops against your legs, there will be a permanent break.

PAINT. A dream of paint depends for its significance upon its color. Look up COLORS (ch. V).

PANSY. Dreaming of a pansy has a decidedly unfortunate augury. It foretells a period during which, for one reason or another, your friends will shun you.

PAPERING. It is an augury of coming misfortune to dream of trying to paper the walls of a room.

PARCEL. A surprise is likely to come after a dream of receiving a parcel by mail or express.

PARSLEY. Petty irritations are to be expected after a dream of seeing food garnished with parsley.

PENDULUM. To see a pendulum swinging in a dream is a sign that you will meet a friend whom you have not seen in many years.

PEACOCK. A disappointment is in store for you if you dream of seeing a peacock. If the tail feathers are spread out, the augury is worse.

PEAS. Canned peas are a sign of a disappointing experience, but green peas augur happiness.

PEN. It prophesies a business enterprise of importance if you dream of using any kind of a pen.
    A pig-pen is an omen of a disagreeable experience.

PEONY. In a dream of peonies, the color is the determining factor. Look up COLORS (ch. V).

PEPPERMINT. Tasting peppermint in a dream denotes pride in the achievements of someone in your immediate family.

**PIER.** Drawing up to a pier in a boat of any kind is a forerunner of the successful outcome of some project you are planning.

**PIG PEN** (*See* Pen).

**PILLS.** You are likely to travel if you dream of taking pills.

**PIMPLES.** Pimples are an omen of illness. To dream of picking them prophesies breaking a leg.

**PITCHFORK.** You will be likely to gain weight through overeating if you dream of using a pitchfork.

**PLAYING CARDS.** In interpreting a dream of playing cards, remember that red is of good omen and black is unfortunate. Ace is high and deuce is low.

Hearts indicate good fortune in love; diamonds stand for wealth.

Spades point to hard work without reward; while clubs portend disgrace.

The higher the cards in the red suits, the better is the augury.

The higher the cards in the black suits, the worse is the augury.

**POCKET.** Beware of the appearance of evil if you dream of putting your hand into someone else's pocket.

**POPPIES.** A dream of poppies foretells a scandalous experience with one of the opposite sex.

**POT.** A chamber pot seen in a dream is an omen of embarrassment.

A cooking pot foretells a vacation amid pleasant surroundings.

To dream of taking the "pot" in a poker game is a sign of success in business.

**POWDER.** You will be deceived by someone in whom you

have put your trust if you dream of using face or talcum powder.

POWER. It is unfortunate to dream of having power to do as you wish. You are likely to fail at something you try to do.

PRAISE. If, in your dream, someone is praising you, it is a forerunner of being blamed for something you have done.
To praise another in a dream foretells success in the work you are doing.

PRIDE. Any show of vain pride in a dream "goeth before a fall."

PRINTING. Hard work that will bring you satisfaction is predicted by a dream of seeing printing done.

PRIZE FIGHT. You are likely to lose money if you dream of witnessing a prize fight. If you dream of taking part in one, whether or not you win, you may look forward to the receipt of money.

PROCESSION. To dream of watching a military or political procession is a portent of a new but unprofitable business venture.

PUDDING. It is a sign of making some easy money in a doubtful manner if you dream of eating pudding. To dream of making this dish is an augury of disappointment.

PULPIT. Unfavorable news may be expected from a dream of a pulpit, either occupied or unoccupied.

PUNISHMENT. To dream of being punished for a misdeed is a portent of unhappiness. If you are doing the punishing, the augury is a good one.

PUSHING. You are warned against mixing in loose company if you dream of pushing people or things.

PUZZLE. Trying to do a puzzle in a dream is a sign that you will be likely to have many irritating experiences, both big and little.

## Q

QUILT. A dream of a patchwork quilt predicts perplexity as to your future course in business or matrimony.

QUINCE. You are likely to be accused of stupidity if you dream of eating quinces.

To dream of making quince jelly is a forerunner of being snubbed by someone in a high position.

Picking quinces from a tree foretells unfulfilled wishes regarding your career.

QUOITS. Pitching quoits foreshadows business difficulties, no matter whether you dream of winning or losing.

## R

RACOON. This animal seen in a dream is a presage of gloomy days through misunderstandings with friends.

RAISINS. Eating raisins in a dream is a sign that you are using the proper tactics in your business, but a warning against placing too much trust in your associates. Go very slowly before making any accusation.

RAPE. To dream of committing or witnessing a rape prophesies a period of business and mental depression.

RASPBERRY. If this fruit is ripe, the color alone makes it of good augury. To dream of raspberries before they are ripe is a presage of trouble.

RAZOR. No good may be expected from a dream of using a razor in any way. It portends separation, unhappiness and pain.

**REBELLION.** If you dream of rebelling against a government or conditions that you believe should be improved, you are in danger of being accused of falseness to a friend.

**RED** *See* Colors, (ch. V).

**REFLECTION.** To dream of seeing your own reflection in a pool of water or in any polished surface, you will be in danger of having stomach trouble.

**RELIGION.** Misfortune is in store for you after a dream of discussing religion with strange people.

**REVENGE.** A dream of taking revenge for a wrong done you is a forerunner of the loss of a valued friend. If you dream of someone else taking revenge on you, it is a presage of a legacy from someone who is not a relative.

**RIBBONS.** It is a warning against too great familiarity with people you have just met to dream of wearing ribbons.

**RIVAL.** If you dream of a rival in business or love, you will hear disquieting news by post or telegraph.

**RINGWORMS.** This is a warning dream. Do not invest any money in a business until you have thoroughly investigated.

**ROPES.** To dream of being bound by ropes, or of binding someone else, is a sign that you will be unable to succeed in your present plans.

**RUBBER.** A dream of stretching rubber of any description foretells that you are in danger of doing a grave injustice to someone.

A woman who dreams of putting on rubber garments or elastic garters should be warned against listening to the gossip of her neighbors.

**RUNNING.** Business conditions will be active but not

profitable if you dream of running.

RUST. If you dream of finding rust on any kind of metal, you are likely to have a hazardous experience of some kind.

<h2 style="text-align:center">S</h2>

SAMPLES. It is a sign that you will engage in some building enterprise if you dream of receiving samples of food, materials or magazines.

For a salesman to dream of packing his samples in a case or trunk is a warning against too much conviviality with his customers.

SAND. To dream of eating sand is usually a forerunner of an automobile or elevator accident. It is a warning to those who drive cars.

SCALDING. Take unusual care to guard against colds if you dream of scalding yourself with any hot liquid.

SCHOOL TEACHER. A variety of worries will be likely to follow a dream of one of your childhood school teachers.

SCUM. A contagious disease is the prophecy of this dream.

SCYTHE. To be mowing with a scythe in a dream foretells the disgrace of one of your friends.

SHAVING. It is an augury of a change of address, either of your home or business, if you dream of shaving any part of the body other than the face.

SHIRT STUDS. A dream of losing a shirt stud under a bureau or other piece of furniture is a warning to guard your temper lest it get you into serious difficulties.

SIEVE. Using a sieve in a dream predicts that you will receive a gift from an older person.

**SKULL.** Some stupid but well-meaning person is liable to make trouble for you if you dream of finding a real skull of a man or woman.

Skulls manufactured for Hallowe'en or other decorative purposes denotes a gay party in the near future.

**SMALLPOX.** This is an omen that you should be more sympathetic toward unfortunate people.

**SNEEZING.** Better health than you now enjoy is predicted by a dream of sneezing.

**SOAP.** The use of soap in a dream, whether on your body or your clothing, is an indication that you will meet with some minor triumph.

Slipping on a cake of soap, either in the bathtub or elsewhere, portends a family row.

**SODA WATER.** It is a sign that you will have a good digestion if you dream of drinking soda.

**SOWING.** To dream of sowing any kind of seeds is a forerunner of business success through careful planning.

**SPECTACLES.** For a person who does not wear glasses to dream of wearing spectacles, there is a warning against ostentation that leads one to buy what he or she cannot afford.

**SPONGE.** You will be likely to lose considerable money if you dream of squeezing water out of a sponge.

**SPOTS.** On clothing, spots are a sign of poor business. If you dream of having them removed, your business will improve.

**SQUINT.** You will be looked up to by your friends if you dream of squinting at people. If other people squint at you, you will be suspected of wrongdoing.

**STAMMERING.** A dream of stammering in the presence

of a person of high rank is an omen that you will be called upon to sign an important document.

STILTS. To dream of walking on stilts is a forerunner of a series of misunderstandings with your associates.

STINK. An unpleasant odor of any kind in a dream is a portent of bad news.

SULPHUR. To dream of burning sulphur is an indication of family worries. Otherwise, see Yellow under COLOR (ch. V).

SUNDIAL. It is probable that you will make a discovery that you can use profitably if you dream of seeing a sundial.

SURF. You may expect a long period of restlessness if you dream of watching the surf at the seashore. If the dream is of bathing or boating in the surf, be warned against taking unnecessary risks.

SWITCH. Someone will cause you great embarrassment if you dream of using a switch on a child.
    You will have to make an important decision if you dream of a railroad switch.
    A woman who dreams of wearing a switch made of hair should be warned against gossiping.

SYRINGE. To use a syringe of any kind in a dream is a sign that a new opportunity is in store for you, and that you should be on the lookout for it.

T

TADPOLES. You are warned against taking part in any conspiracy if you have this dream, for tadpoles are a sign of defeat.

TAILOR. For a man or woman to dream of being measured

by a tailor signifies that he or she will be harassed by jealous persons.

TAPEWORM. Money that you have expected to receive will be delayed if you dream of having this affliction.

TAPROOM (*See* Barroom).

TAXICAB. If in a dream you are riding alone in a taxicab, it foretells an achievement that will bring you considerable money. To dream of being in a taxicab with a person of the opposite sex is a warning against indiscreet behavior.

TEACHER (*See* School Teacher).

TELESCOPE. A journey is predicted by seeing distant objects through a telescope. You will be disappointed if you dream of looking through the wrong end.

THATCHED ROOF. Great care should be exercised after this dream to guard against accidents.

THUMB. It is an augury of an unpleasant surprise to dream of having a person put his thumb to his nose in a gesture of scorn. If you dream of doing it yourself, you will be lucky in a business deal.

TIARA. A woman who dreams of wearing a jeweled tiara will be accused of keeping shameful company.

TOAD. This is a warning not to engage in any business or social transaction that will not bear the closest scrutiny.

TOAST. Burned toast, smelled or eaten in a dream, is a sign that you will lose a friend through carelessness.

TOBOGGAN. To ride on a toboggan slide in a dream is an omen that you will succeed in the accomplishment of your ambition after many difficulties.

**TORRENT.** If you dream of being caught in a torrent, or a torrential rain, you will have to defend yourself against an accusation of hypocrisy.

**TRAILER.** To dream of traveling or camping with a trailer to an automobile is a happy augury for men but not for women. A man having this dream may reasonably expect a long period of contentment, while for a woman it predicts the opposite.

**TROUSERS.** A laughable experience is in store for you if you dream of seeing a woman wearing trousers. To see a man without trousers, but otherwise clad, betokens sadness.

**TURKISH BATH.** To dream of being in a Turkish bath is a forerunner of an unexpected trip to a distant point, although not of necessity into a foreign land.

**TURNIPS.** Illness is predicted if you dream of eating these vegetables.

**TURTLE.** It is bad luck to dream of seeing a turtle turned over on its back.

**TWINE.** Tangled twine is an omen of problems that will take a long time to solve. If it is neatly wound in a ball, it augurs a period of calm.

# U

**UNCLE.** This dream portends that you will doubt one of your good friends. The warning is that you should not doubt unjustly.

**UNDRESSED.** To dream of finding yourself undressed in a public place foretells that you will receive an unexpected honor.

**URN.** A merely decorative urn is a portent of gloom. A coffee urn, or one used for other practical purposes, presages happiness.

# V

**VARNISH.** If in a dream you sit on a newly varnished piece of furniture, it predicts that you will be cheated by a dishonest tradesman.

**VAT.** You will be called upon to explain your actions if you dream of falling into a vat of any kind.
   Business success is predicted by a dream of mixing substances in a vat.

**VENEER.** A well-mannered person will seek to deceive you after a dream of seeing the veneer peeling off an article of furniture.

**VENTRILOQUIST.** You will be able to help a friend who is in trouble if you dream of hearing a ventriloquist.

**VICE.** To dream of indulging in one or more vices is a sign that you will attain popularity in social life.

**VIOLIN** (*See* Music, ch. V).

**VOLCANO.** In eruption, a volcano is a sign of failure. It presages death to a near relative. An extinct volcano is an omen of sickness to one of your friends.

**VOMIT.** This is a fortunate augury, especially to those who are sick or unhappy.

**VOTING.** Going to the polls in a dream is a forerunner of meeting an influential person who will take an interest in your welfare.

**VULTURE.** This is a bird of ill omen. To dream of one denotes that you will have difficulty in business.

# W

**WAGER.** To dream of making a bet is a distinct warning not to do so for at least a month.

**WAIL.** Someone will seek to betray a woman who dreams of hearing a wail, whether of a human being or an animal.

**WAITER OR WAITRESS.** It is a sign that one of your acquaintances will tell you lies if you dream of being waited on in a restaurant.

**WALL.** Climbing over a wall in a dream is an omen of surmounting a difficulty.

**WARBLING.** To dream of birds warbling foretells sickness in your family.

**WAR.** If a man dreams of going to war, he should guard his actions in regard to his behavior toward women.

**WASHBOARD.** This dream is a forerunner of difficulty in making ends meet financially.

**WASTE.** A dream of wasting food or money is, as might be expected, an omen of want. If the dream concerns wasting time, the omen is of disappointment.

**WAVES.** (*See* Surf).

**WAX CANDLES.** Beware of designing women or men.

**WEASEL.** If you dream of a weasel, you will find it difficult to make people believe in you.

**WEAVING.** To work at a loom in a dream is a warning against placing too much trust in strangers.

**WEEDING.** You are likely to be disappointed in someone

you believed to be a friend if you dream of pulling or hoeing weeds.

WELSH RAREBIT. To dream of enjoying Welsh rarebit is a forerunner of grief through an accident.

WET NURSE. For an unmarried woman to dream that she is a wet nurse is a warning against being guided by other people's advice against her better judgment. For a married woman, the dream means happiness.

WHEELS (*See* Cars).

WHIP (*See* Switch).

WHIRLPOOL (*See* Torrent).

WHISTLE. It is bad luck to hear a whistle of any kind in a dream. It portends some sort of calamity.

WOLF. If you dream of one or more wolves, it is a sign that someone is trying to jeopardize your position.

WORKING. If, in your dream of working, you appear to be making progress, the portent is a good one for your success. On the other hand, if the work is tedious and unproductive, you will suffer a disappointment.

WRECK. It is an augury of accident to dream of a wreck of any kind, whether on land or sea.

WRITING. Anyone who dreams of writing for publication will be likely to suffer disillusionment in connection with their ambitions.

# X

XYLOPHONE. Hearing and seeing an expert performer on this instrument is a dream of achieving an ambition with honour.

# Y

**YARDSTICK.** Measuring articles with a yardstick in a dream is a sign that you are too critical of your friends.

**YAWNING.** If, in your dream, you yawn while another person is present, be on the lookout for fraudulent practices by business houses.

**YOUTH.** This is a dream of pleasant augury unless you see and hear young people quarreling.

# Z

**ZULU.** A dream of seeing Zulus in their native environment engaged in peaceful pursuits is a sign that you will be able to smooth out your immediate difficulties.

## INDEX
## OF DREAMS, ETC.

271

272

275

276

Gypsy, 100

## H

## I

278

280

## O

## P

282